W9-DDE-792

Energy Tools have helped me understand the relationship between energy and physical pain. My ability to help myself and my patients heal has increased significantly.

~ Dr. K.C., Chiropractor, Seattle, WA

Thanks to this information, I've learned how to keep from feeling others' pain while staying compassionate toward them. I feel less drained, more caring, and I'm not worrying about my patients when I leave work.

~ Barbara J., Nurse, Yakima, WA

These tools have helped me realize my life was being directed by other people's wants, not my own. Now I'm creating the work I want and am financially enjoying my life.

~ Steve G., Real Estate Broker, Atlanta, GA

Working with the energy tools in Spirit Matters gave me the courage to end a marriage of 47 years of abuse. Using the energy tools, I was able to stabilize myself physically and mentally through a very stressful time of leaving home and stable income behind. I stopped thinking that I am too old (70); it's too late to change; it is just easier to die. Can I have a new life? I am creating each day with a fresh breath and new hope. That was two years ago. Today I use those same tools to bring myself back to better physical and emotional heath by clearing out the debris of unwanted memories in order to find happiness again. Thank you, Roxane.

~ Pat N., New York

Dear Roxane and Jim,

For the past several weeks I have been fighting a kind of "unknown" illness. Unknown because even a trip to the emergency room and a traditional doctor could not pinpoint exactly what is ailing me. All they could do was issue prescriptions for stomach cramps and nausea and feed me anti-biotics "in case of an infection."

All of these pills have done little to help, and have only left my head in a fog. So, lately I have turned to the more holistic healing tools I learned through you. Relaxing in the Center of My Head and Running My Energy have helped me to feel more rested and less plagued by the varying symptoms of my illness.

I know there are those who would argue that this is a silly notion, but I am writing to you to refute the nay-sayers. As yours is a very holistic notion of mental and physical health, being in touch with your Spiritual Self is the first step in maintaining a healthy life. Exercises like Grounding and Running Energy help keep the spirit in the physical body, therefore making it easier to heal.

Once the body is made aware of these tools and how to use them, it begins to feel better. Being in control of my body is very empowering. This is especially important for women, who have been subject to the whims of doctors and researchers who have little concept of what our bodies go through on a regular basis. To be in control of one's own health is a very welcome change.

I want to thank you for the gifts you have given me. I feel that I am stronger and healthier because of the tools you gave me. I wish that there were a way to help others come to this realization.

No effort would be too small if it helps to spread these tools to others who need a little spiritual guidance. Their health and well being may depend upon it. I know mine did.

With sincere appreciation,

A. Monroe

Extraordinary! These energy tools are both practical and profound. What I have learned has allowed me to transform chronic issues and to create realities that I didn't think were possible.

~ Susan B., Retired Bank Executive, Atlanta GA

I look forward to each chapter very much. So much is happening...so very fast. I can feel the veil physically lifting every day, and as it lifts, the vision of heaven on earth becomes less of a dream and more of a reality. It is exciting to be here at this time. I am so grateful for your commitment to this. Thank you, thank you.

~ Joyce V., CFO, Miami FL

The tools have allowed me to understand how my decision making was affected by other people's energy. My business is now back on track. These tools really work!

~ Bill W., CEO, San Jose, CA

Jim - Your energy tools have literally changed my life! I now am confident in my actions and decisions; I no longer choose based on fear of what others may think or do -- I KNOW that my decisions are best for me and my goals. The energy tools have helped me create job opportunities and all the resources I need to fulfill my dreams.

~ Dr. Gail L., Minneapolis, MN

Spirit Matters
Down-to-Earth Tools for a Spirited Life

Jim Self
Roxane Burnett

First Printing, 2002
Second Printing, 2003
Third Printing, 2003
Fourth Printing, 2006

Second Edition Printing, 2008

Cover Design Gratitude to:
Yulia Rogojnikova. www.yvrgraphics.com

Every story printed here is absolutely true.
Some people have asked for anonymity.

Published by:
Tree of Life Press

Represented by
Mastering Alchemy: www.MasteringAlchemy.com
and
Transition Coaching for Women:
www.TransitionCoachingForWomen.com

ISBN 0-9718650-2-7

Printed in the United States of America
by Fidlar Doubleday.

▲

Dedicated to those who ask and allow.

▼

▲

Contents

▲

WE THANK YOU

... the students who asked so persistently and waited so patiently.
... our co-creators including:

Cynthia Schutt
Michelle Supelana-Mix
Lynette Garron
Yulia Rogojnikova
Denise Swenson
Shirley Rawson
Metatron
Mother Mary
Saint Germaine

▲

Overview by Jim

How to Enjoy tHE SHift

The world we have created is a product of our thinking.
It cannot be changed without changing our thinking.

Albert Einstein

There is a change, a "Shift" under way that is affecting every aspect of our third dimensional reality. This Shift is so far-reaching that our limited imagination cannot begin to grasp the transition and change we are now in the midst of experiencing.

This Shift is affecting every aspect of life on the planet; political, social and economic structures, the environment, every institutional system, the wars, how we view our relationships, our work, every thought we think and every feeling we feel.

It is altering Time, our memory, our DNA, the wiring of our physical and emotional bodies, our beliefs, our perceptions of good and bad, right and wrong and especially our awareness of what is possible.

The Shift is composed of huge waves of Light which hold massive amounts of information and instructions. These waves are re-wiring our DNA, providing new electromagnetic frequencies to upgrade the body's physical, emotional and mental systems. These waves of Light are activating the fourth and fifth dimensional chakras, aligning us with a higher awareness.

This Shift is providing new understandings of how to once again live in harmony with each other, the environment and All That Is. However, between this new "Heaven on Earth" and where we currently exist, there is transition.

The Transition

This transition, as exciting and wonderful as it is, is creating difficulties for many. These difficulties are occurring as the pace of the Shift quickens, but we continue to hold our third dimensional beliefs and way of life as truths. We continue to argue for the right and wrongs, judge others for their actions or fix them because "we know better." These actions belong to the third dimension and they must be released. As long as we continue to hold these limitations, we will experience the affects of this Shift within our physical and emotional bodies. These affects are becoming known as "Ascension Symptoms."

These symptoms can manifest as dizziness, confusion, loss of focus, headaches, fatigue and increased tiredness, digestion discomfort, anxiety, nervousness, etc. You are experiencing Time going faster. There is more on our plate and less time to complete it. (See Chapter 11.) We are losing aspects of our memories (no, it's not Alzheimer's). Things that were once very important are no longer as important. And most of us are feeling a heightened sense of distraction coupled with an emotional sense that something is just not right. As we argue for our limitations and hold on to the old beliefs which no longer support us, we create a resistance or blockage within our four-body system, creating these discomforts.

The third dimensional reality as we have known it is shifting. It is becoming far more grand, aligned and balanced, moving into a Higher Consciousness. Humanity is waking up and as it does, the old structures that have supported duality, maintained separation and controlled the masses with fear are crumbling.

As this new Light finds its way into every corner of darkness on the Planet, those that live within the darkness are beginning to recoil, react and become very noisy. They will scream the loudest to maintain the status quo. They are creating distraction, wars, economic failures, and many other distractions to prevent this Shift from occurring. They will, for a short time, become very loud, generating much fear in their attempt to avoid this Shift. They have already failed, AND they will be very noisy.

As this new Light flows within each of us, we are now receiving new information, opportunities and choices which were not available to us in the past. These choices are now allowing each of us to step out of the fear, distraction and separation.

By grounding, realigning your energy fields and stabilizing your attention point and focus, you will make the bodies SAFE during the noise. The Tools in this book will assist you in doing this.

Grounding

Grounding is something almost everyone has thought about or considered. But grounding is not a thought; it is an action, a tool to dissipate noisy thoughts, anxiety and undesirable emotions that run through our bodies. From my perspective, this tool is the most valuable. (See Chapter Two.)

The Octahedron

Surrounding you are a number of energy fields, one of which you know as the aura or Etheric body. The aura gathers, retains and files every thought, word and action that occurs within, through and around you. In other words, it holds a lot of information, much of which has very little to do with you. This energy field is also an antenna. It attracts frequencies of thought.

If you can manage the antenna, you can manage what the antenna attracts. Constructing this antenna around you creates a powerful energy field which aligns with the information of the Shift and your own internal guidance system. In Sacred Geometry there are five forms, known as Platonic Solids, which hold unique characteristics. One is the Octahedron. It is one four-sided pyramid pointing up with a second four-sided pyramid connected at the base and pointing down. (See Chapter Ten.)

Building and holding the Octahedron creates a sense of containment. This containment is not a wall or a defense system; it is a safe vessel that allows you to move around without becoming affected by the noise. It is also an antenna which aligns with the Light and Infinite Intelligence being transmitted during this Shift. The Octahedron creates an alignment with all that you are and simply filters out that which you are not.

Experience and play with these two tools and the many others we offer you here. As simple as they are, they will alter your conscious reality and allow you to enjoy the flow of the Shift.

May you experience love and laughter on your journey Home.

Jim

▲

Introduction by Roxane

tHE How And WHy

The tools and information we are about to share with you have changed the lives of many thousands of people. They are "standard equipment" accompanying the vehicle you call your body, much like the tires and horn that come with your new car. These tools exist in your Spiritual Toolbox, which unfortunately, came with no instruction manual, nor even a description of contents. Once rediscovered, however, your body, mind and emotions recognize and remember a way of operating that creates greater well-being, joy and health. Your Spirit, your essential self, can then safely step out of hiding and truly express passion, certainty and amusement, its true creative purpose.

I discovered these tools in 1994. I had left the East Coast, my corporate job and my husband. I left because I was dying. I was in so much pain and felt so disconnected from who I was that I prayed daily to die. I prayed for cancer. I prayed for every deadly disease I could think of. Because I believed suicide was not a wise spiritual move, I opted for disease. I helped the death process along by drinking massive quantities of alcohol to become numb every day for three years. I self-medicated because to remain sober and conscious in my pain was more than I believed I could handle. It wasn't until a close friend on the West Coast died in September, 1993, that I brought together my Selves, my sub-personalities as I called them back then, and came to an internal agreement to leave. It was the day after Thanksgiving.

I was sitting on the living room floor, wrapping Christmas gifts for my husband's family. He was in the kitchen. It was 11a.m. and, surprisingly enough, I wasn't completely drunk yet. The voices in my head became louder. They told me to return "Home." I knew the mail had arrived downstairs and I spontaneously made a deal with God. If there was any mail from California, even junk mail, I would take it as a sign that I was to return there to begin again. I had previously spent many years in Northern California, prior to meeting my husband and moving to his parents' house in Delaware. I walked down the stairs and found my destiny. Not only did I receive mail from California, but discovered it was a beautiful card from my dead friend's lover.

It took me another three months to actually gather enough money to set off. Although I had a well-paying job as an advertising director in Pennsylvania, I had no money of my own. It was during these three months that I was daily challenged to hold to my Truth. My husband and his family thought I would change my mind and see what a good boy he was. My supervisor thought I would change my mind and see how foolish I was to think I could get a job in "economically depressed" California. Everyone knew I'd fail miserably. I experienced fear like I never had before. I was jumping off a cliff and knew not where I would land, or if I would land safely. I did know jumping was my only true option. Some people thought I was courageous and brave. I was neither. I was driven. Until you jump off a few cliffs in life, you think it takes courage. It doesn't. Instead, the motivation is an interesting mix of fear and trust. One who jumps learns to talk to her Self and do what she is told.

I safely landed in a fifth-wheel trailer in the backyard of a friend's and took three comfortable months to find my feet. I then, "synchronistically", obtained a rare and ideal art director position. I also met Jim who introduced me to these Energy Tools. They changed my life. The little hippy-chick, victim, hiding behind her fear, frumpy clothes and long fuzzy hair disappeared and grew into a teacher of tools, counselor and coach. No psychotherapy or twelve-step program was necessary. Instead, balance was established from a foundation of true Personal Power. As my whole system became balanced emotionally, mentally and physically, the life force and passionate spirit within me had a safe, permissive environment to fly. Xenophobia was no longer an issue. Presence and Certainty became mine. All that was required was commitment to my Self and the desire to follow my path and passion, my "Personal Legend" as Paulo Coelho describes in *The Alchemist*. (1)

I am now blessed to be one of those people who does what she loves. I got here from the use of the tools I now present to you. The tools and techniques are designed to reflect "kindergarten" eagerness and ease. Kindergartners feel as though they can do anything. They are seldom serious. Do you remember those times?

My goal and deepest desire is to offer you the inspiration, safety and permission to jump off your cliffs and become who you truly are. This information is for all who long for empowerment and personal freedom. For you, I'll share everything I know and am.

To Life Immortal!

Rx

Although we co-authored this work, we thought it would be easier and smoother for you to read, comprehend and experience if we kept the information and stories in the first person, rather than continually moving between identifying who contributed which pieces.

With Eyes and Ears

Energy Tools are not an intellectual process.
They are an experiential journey.

T hose of us who originally learned these mental image tools did so through the verbal tradition of the "Ancient Mystery Schools." We received nothing in print and many of us wrote copious volumes of notes after class, which usually ended at 10 p.m. three nights a week. Our teachers never drew diagrams or tolerated note-taking during class. That method worked for us then, but today a great number of people all over the world are asking for, even demanding, this information.

Receiving new information via the spoken word is a much different experience than reading it. Hearing the instructions stimulates a part of your brain that reading does not, and vica-versa. Reading tends to be a more analytical or intellectual process than simply following along as someone tells you what to do. Reading these procedures may not be the most effective method of experiencing these Energy Tools, but it's the method most available.

This is an experiential journey. It is a journey of inner and outer transformation. If you are inspired to experiment with the tools, read the written instructions into a tape recorder and use the recording to more fully experience their power. Be sure to leave plenty of blank tape between each step so you may have time to perform the exercises.

▲

Chapter One
A Master Thinker

The world we have created is a product of our thinking.
It cannot be changed without changing our thinking.

Albert Einstein

Thought can be our greatest ability. It can also be our greatest liability. Our thought creates our experience of the world. Wilber and Orville Wright knew this. Nikola Tesla's thoughts evolved into alternating current. Alexander Bell turned his thoughts into the telephone. Tesla, Wilber, Orville and Bell, were able to hold their thoughts upon their dreams long enough and strong enough to bring them into solid form. That's the only difference between the successful ones and those who struggle and never quite make it. It is the degree to which they intentionally think and then focus upon what they think.

Your thoughts are creating 24 hours a day. In fact, everything you are currently experiencing in this moment, in your relationship, in your job, in your town began as a thought. This tool called *thought* is a powerful, sharp sword that we usually wield as if it were a wild, out of control garden hose, splashing everyone and everything around us with something that can be uncomfortable, wet and certainly not well-directed. Intentional, directed thoughts always result in clear, manageable outcomes. Do you remember the last time you were involved in a consuming, exciting, creative project? When you completed this project you were quite likely proud of yourself and knew you'd done a great job. There may have been ups and downs, even surprises, but the journey was always one of enjoyment and creative passion. You knew that you were on the right track. The goal was always out in front of you and you could easily imagine it. The finished product may have actually been quite different than what you first imagined, but it was probably much better than anticipated!

Although we are creating 24 hours a day, we are not usually creating with intentionality or with a specific direction and goal. In fact, we can be extremely sloppy thinkers. What does sloppy thinking produce? Sloppy thoughts always produce sloppy, unsatisfying results. Many times sloppy thinking results in feelings of being overwhelmed of helplessness and of victimization. There is sometimes a sense of just trying to "keep up." Putting out fires is no longer creative, glamorous or thrilling. Have you ever experienced a job you didn't enjoy or an uncomfortable relationship or an uncomfortable body? If we could trace back from your present-time experience, whether preferred or not preferred, we would find an original thought that produced it. And – this original thought wasn't idle and uncharged. This thought had punch. It held so much punch that it created the situation you find yourself in today. It was also not alone. There were other similar thoughts surrounding and supporting it. Like attracts like, and like a magnet, these thoughts (intentional or sloppy) attract others like them. Have you ever had the experience of going through a personal crisis, let's say a relationship separation, and you found several others in your life going through a similar thing?

Or have you ever deliberately, even obsessively, tried to avoid something only to have it happen anyway? When we think a strong thought, bundled with emotion, about what we don't want, we get it. That's sloppy thinking. Intentional thinking is the art of directing your uncluttered thoughts toward the thing you *do* want to create in your life. When an adult tells a young child, "Don't spill the milk," what usually happens? The child spills the milk. Why? In order to know what, "Don't spill the milk," is like, the child must first think about and visualize spilling the milk. And when he thinks about spilling the milk, there usually is a strong emotional charge about it (a fear of the consequences). So the thought of spilling is so strong and so charged, the child does exactly what he was trying to avoid.

You've had the experience of strongly resisting or avoiding someone you don't care for, have unfinished business with, or whom you simply feel uncomfortable around. You hope you don't bump into them and perhaps even check every curve to see if they're there, so you can quickly turn the other way. Then, suddenly, they show up right next to you in a line or you bump into them at the store, again and again. You want so strongly to *not* see them, and now seeing them is unavoidable. When you have a thought in your mind, especially if is accompanied with an emotion, that thought is magnetically attracted to you, whether you truly want it or not.

●●●

Donald had recurring thoughts that his wife, just like all the women before her, was going to leave him. This fearful thought carried a strong emotional charge and was in his conscious awareness so frequently, it became a belief. This belief of being abandoned eventually revealed itself through Donald's words and behavior until after seven years of continued fear and expectation of rejection in his marriage, Donald created a situation where his very loyal wife left him. His behavior evolved into verbal abuse directed at her. This continued to push her away sexually and emotionally, until, in order for her to survive, she had to leave him. Perhaps you know a Donald in your life?

• • •

These sloppy, self-destructive thoughts don't just occur overnight. Donald didn't instantly fear abandonment. You didn't just suddenly find yourself fearing confrontation, feeling self-conscious or hiding. You were not suddenly unfulfilled at work or in life. Single, individual thoughts slowly, over many years, build upon each other to become belief patterns and then behavior patterns. And do you know what? These thoughts were never yours to begin with. They belonged to your family, your culture, and the entire vortex you live in.

Becoming an intentional, Master Thinker is quite revolutionary. In fact intentional thinking is not generally encouraged. Intentional, independent thinkers are sometimes labeled troublemakers and problem students. Kids with a strong spirit and clear agenda are told to behave themselves and fit in. It is sometimes difficult for the surrounding adults to manage and control intentional thinkers. Our parents, working from the old patterning of their parents, told us how to grow up and be successful, healthy and happy. They told us to follow the rules, control ourselves, fit in and be a productive part of society. They wanted the best for their children and that meant creating a life *they* believed was good for us.

It requires commitment and attention to understand ones own truth, let alone allow your child to discover hers. Guiding and encouraging children is a great challenge for all parents. Have you ever known a mother who encourages her child to jump into the deep end of the pool, take a risk or stub his toe? There aren't many parents who allow their kids to bump around and figure out life for themselves. When the child falls off his bicycle, what generally happens? The parent runs over to pick him up and fix him. Many parents continue to pick up their adult children's bicycles and then complain that the kids are too dependent upon them! Many adults are just now learning how to pick up their own bikes and don't know the first thing about how to love themselves and create their lives. We have been thinking others' thoughts and consequently living others' dreams for so long, we have forgotten which dreams are ours and what rules really work for us. What are we mentoring to our children? Only our truths? Or are we creating the safety and permission for them to tip over their bicycles and discover their own individual truths, becoming the intentional thinkers they were born to be?

Thought is the bottom line. As one thinks, so one experiences. Jim Self, High Performance Coach and seminar leader, puts it this way:

> *Culture is created by group agreements. Group agreements are based upon beliefs. Beliefs are simply thoughts that are repeated. Therefore if we change our individual thoughts, we change the culture.*

Culture can be universal, planetary, hemispheric, national, local, business, social, religious or family structure. The condition of the culture is determined by the group agreements, as well as the beliefs and thoughts each member of the culture is repeating and embracing, individually.

As you become a Master Thinker, you will experience shifts and changes in your life. You will experience enhanced emotional balance. Your moods swing less; you become satisfied and happy, passionate and peaceful. You will experience mental clarity, less noise and increased focus. Your ability to use both analytical processes and your intuitive skills becomes greater and more aligned. Physically, you have more energy and ease; your body feels healthier and alive. When you become the master of your thoughts, your mental, emotional and physical aspects come into balance and another pretty incredible thing happens. Automatically and effortlessly, you have created the room and safety for the creative surge and passion of your true Spirit to begin to express itself. Your creative genius in unleashed. And this all happens when you simply master your thoughts. *As we think, so we experience.*

Experience the Power of Your Thought

Would you like to play with your thoughts and undeniably experience how powerful they are? This is an example of how a simple thought can influence your body. Please just read each instruction, then close your eyes and experience the effect.

1. Think of a lemon. Focus on the memory of a ripe, juicy, bright and luscious lemon. Imagine its color and texture. It feels cool to the touch and the skin is smooth with many tiny dimples. Really visualize the lemon.

2. Now imagine cutting the lemon in half. Watch the knife slowly slide through it and notice the pulp burst. Notice the drops of juice rolling down the blade of the knife.

3. Now visualize scraping your front teeth across the open, juicy pulp of this lemon. Take in the full experience of the tiny pockets of juice bursting and exploding in your mouth.

4. Really imagine this experience. Also, please notice the response of your body. Are your saliva glands stimulated? Are your shoulders tense? Take a breath.

You were just sitting there, having a very simple, common thought and your body responded. What if you took the power of your thought and directed it, not at a lemon, but at your relationship, career or health. That thought, so clearly and powerfully focused upon the simple lemon caused an effect in your physical reality. Your thought can equally affect anything else you direct it upon. What would you like to focus upon?

Have you ever participated in a firewalk? On December 31, 1997 I attended a New Year's celebration firewalk. It wasn't about walking on burning coals (which we did). It was about the power of thought. If you can master your thoughts and believe that 2,000-degree coals won't damage the flesh on your feet, you can do anything. About 100 of us attended that night. After a series of exercises that challenged mind, body, emotions and spirit, we held our thoughts and beliefs and walked. Most of us walked several times. Bette, a beginning Energy Tools student, had a validating experience. She was on her third stroll over the white coals when she suddenly slipped and fell. She landed face up, sitting on the coals, leaning on her hands. The other participants, standing on either side of the 6 foot by 20 foot glowing track, gasped and began to quickly move toward her, obviously convinced she was about to ignite into a giant flame. They were ready to pull her out to safety. Bette remained seated where she was and waved the others back, away from her. She slowly crawled her way up to a standing position again, calmly continued her walk and completed it with only a very small "kiss" on the palm of one hand. No bit of clothing or hair was burned and Bette was congratulated royally at the end of her walk. If she had broken her belief of Certainty, Bette would not have fared so well. It was only her strong belief in her well-being that kept her safe, unharmed and unaffected. Had she matched the others' beliefs and fears and let them affect her, the fire would have certainly caused some damage. It was the power of her thought that kept Bette safe.

The condition of your body, your business and every aspect of your life is determined by the thoughts you think. Become a Master Thinker and begin to master your life.

To become a Master Thinker, first you must identify and release the tired or even harmful thoughts that no longer benefit you. Then, you must replace those thoughts with ones that do benefit you. Sound simple? It is. However, it may not be so easy sometimes because there is a huge wave of conditioning and habit that you are pushing against when you begin to take back command of your thoughts and your life. Heaven forbid – you may become an independent thinker, an unmanageable renegade and a troublemaker.

Are you ready to become a troublemaker??

Chapter Two

Hearing the Flute

In a world of noise, confusion and conflict it is necessary that there be a place of silence, inner discipline and peace.

Thomas Merton

To become a Master Thinker, you must first recognize the thoughts currently bumping around in your head. This doesn't mean you must change the thoughts; just notice them. Be aware of them. These thoughts are the foundation that supports and creates the beliefs, behavior and experiences in your life. Becoming aware of your thoughts causes you to step out of them briefly to observe them, somewhat like a scientist, studying a strange new life form. This stepping out of the thought pattern disrupts your relationship with it and begins to neutralize any emotional, mental or physical charge that may be attached to the thought. You quickly become a neutral and amused observer, simply watching an interesting movie.

Once we begin to notice our thoughts, many of us immediately get overwhelmed by the noise in our heads. And the more we try to quiet the noise, the louder it screams. The louder it screams, the more discouraged we get with the entire process. Eventually we get so distracted by the strongest, loudest concern, we forget what we were doing. If you have ever tried to meditate using any of the traditional or popular mind-quieting methods, you've probably experienced this phenomenon. The more you attempt to quiet that monkey on the chain, the louder it screeches and the more it runs around.

In order to successfully notice your thoughts, it's important to first move some of the noise out. Do you have noise or chatter in your life? Or a committee in your head? How about an entire orchestra? Sometimes it's as if you're listening to a complex piece of classical music that includes many instruments playing simultaneously. You'd like to isolate and enjoy just the flute, but the violins, horns, and drums are the only instruments you hear. How do you quiet what you don't want to pay attention to, in order to hear what you do want? Have you ever returned home from a busy day at work and found yourself playing with the kids, but still thinking about work? Have you ever finally made it to bed at the end of the day and still hear a conversation with someone going on in your head? Or perhaps you have night-dreams of working. If left to their own devices, that noise can become loud and annoying and interfere with your concentration, performance and life. It can affect your entire system, including your emotions (anxiety), mental clarity (confusion) and physical balance (illness). Wouldn't it be great to quiet the noise so you could concentrate and focus on what you *do* enjoy?

The first Energy Tool I'd like to introduce is extremely simple and effective in quieting your mind. It can eliminate stress and allow you to take back your Certainty. This "Grounding Line" is a device that brings your body and mind back into ease. I've watched this tool align and rebalance people of all persuasions: professionals, business people, sports pros and young children alike.

This tool is not new. It has existed in various forms and has been called many things throughout time. It is an important aspect in many spiritual practices. Your body comes with standard physical equipment such as fingers and toes. It also comes with non-physical or energy equipment. The Grounding Line is one of these. All it requires is a little thought.

Energy Tool #1
Grounding Line

1. Recognize when your mind is being bombarded with uncomfortable thoughts. This may sound like an obvious first step, but most people do not pay attention to what is going in their heads and continue to be affected by the chatter. There is a one-to-one relationship between mind and body, balance and imbalance. When the mind is noisy or uncertain, the body is tight and anxious.

2. Find a quiet, undisturbed place to sit down for a few moments. The front seat of your car or the bathroom stall at the office work great too.

3. Breathe. A simple, deep breath will begin to effortlessly change the direction of your thoughts. Your body will begin to quiet. One intentional breath will assist you in returning to a state of neutrality so the intrusive thoughts will begin to lose their grip on you.

4. Bring your attention to the lowest tip of your spine (your coccyx bone). Now is the time to pretend, imagine or make-believe as you did when you were a child. Imagine a line connecting the lower tip of your spine to the center of the earth (it's not that far away). This line could be a beam of light, a tree trunk, a chain, a rope or any image that you find amusing.

5. Strongly secure the Grounding Line at both ends. You may visualize welding it, stapling it, tying it or any other method of attaching.

6.   Now be aware of your feet on the ground. Create a sensation that your feet are cemented to the earth. Feel connected to the earth through your feet and the Grounding Line. Take a couple of breaths. Notice if you have a sense of feeling solid, or taller, or more certain about yourself. Notice if your awareness has become more defined.

7.   Pretend to widen your Grounding Line to a diameter of six to nine inches. You are creating a pathway through which the noise will soon be leaving.

8.   Give the instruction to this Grounding Line to become magnetic. You also might pretend there is a switch or handle near the lower tip of your spine that when flipped, will activate the line. When activated, the Grounding Line will automatically begin to magnetically attract the unpleasant thoughts, physical sensations and emotions and draw them down, out of your space, into the earth. This step works best when you don't try to make it happen. Rather, just allow it to do its job.

9.   As you notice specific people, thoughts and concerns passing through your mind, simply grab them with your imaginary hand and toss them down your Grounding Line. These don't belong to you and they will be much happier in their own heads.

The Grounding Line will automatically do what it is programmed to do. You have to *do* nothing. In fact, the more you *do*, the less this will work. Just pretend, and allow your body to relax back into its natural state of ease.

Added benefits of the Grounding Line

In addition to removing noisy thoughts and feelings from your system and energy field, the Grounding Line brings your thoughts and attention back to the present moment so you may appreciate your environment. Keeping your attention and thoughts in the present moment instead of in the future or past (or even in the next room) is extremely beneficial in managing your life experience.

How can you deal with what's on your plate now, if your attention is on tomorrow's meeting? How can you enjoy the moment if your thoughts are on yesterday's conversation? Grounding that noise helps you enjoy the feast and fun that is spread before you now.

The Grounding Line also lowers your center of gravity. You may want to experiment with this. Attach your Line and begin to slowly walk around. You may notice a more solid feeling in your body. Sometimes people say their legs feel more steady. Many golfers claim the Grounding Line is the Energy Tool they value most, especially in their pre-shot routine. Averages of two strokes have been taken off their scores by using this tool (along with a few others explained later).

> ### Grounding Hint
> Attach a Grounding Line to your pets, children, car, and computer. The Grounding Line grounds out and re-balances static, noise and emotional charge, much like the third prong on an electrical plug.

The Grounding Line prevents you from physically losing balance. In other words, if you have your line well attached and someone physically bumps into you, it will be less likely that you lose your balance and topple over.

When to use the Grounding Line

– First thing in the morning, as you prepare for your day, take a few moments and connect this line. You may attach and use your Grounding Line 24 hours a day. In fact, that is what I recommend. It's a great way to begin your day and set the tone for your daily goals and schedule. It only takes a few moments. You can even do it in the car, as you're driving, however, it's best if you spend a few moments focused just on this work.

– Freshen up your Grounding Line prior to stepping into a charged situation. Don't wait until the chaos is happening around you to use this tool. Check in with it prior to a conversation, meeting, phone call or entering a store. Malls are excellent places to use your Grounding Line.

   – Clear your office, car, home, or any room by Grounding it. Visualize a Grounding Line attached to the upper four and lower four corners of the room and give them the direction to drain any energy from the room that isn't in sync with you.

David Kundts, author of *Stopping: How to Be Still When You Have to Keep Going,* refers to moments of Grounding as "stillpoints" or "mind-clearing breaks." He suggests weaving in 15-20 stillpoints throughout the day, as you are waiting for traffic or in a checkout line. When you're stuck on hold or waiting for the fax machine. (2) Simply take a moment to check in with your Grounding Line and imagine it flushing down any anxiety, worry or other uncomfortable sensation you may be feeling.

●●●

Several years ago I arrived at the Sacramento Airport for a noon flight to Atlanta, Georgia. I was scheduled to present a two-day seminar beginning the next morning. When I stepped up to the check-in counter and presented my ticket, the agent began to robotically tell me, as she typed, "Your flight has been canceled due to mechanical problems. The next flight to Atlanta is scheduled for 10 p.m. and will be arriving at 4 a.m." I was to begin teaching at 8 a.m. and couldn't quite believe what I was hearing so I asked her to repeat what she'd just said. Without looking up from her keyboard, the agent began repeating the identical information she just delivered. This time however, I pretended I was attaching a Grounding Line to her computer. No longer than three seconds into attaching the Grounding Line, the agent interrupted herself and added, "Oh wait, there appears to be one seat now open on the one o'clock flight. Would you like that seat?"

"Oh yes, thank you," I quickly replied, thinking, "This stuff really works." The other impatient passengers were not too happy about my getting the last seat, but hey, they didn't have a Grounding Line. They couldn't hear the flute either!

▲

Chapter Three
Cleaning the Kitchen

It's my conviction that slight shifts in imagination have more impact on living than major efforts at change.

Thomas Moore

As children and adults, you've been given instructions on how to keep your bodies fit and your intellect keen. In fact, it is of extreme value in this culture to be healthy and smart; it's part of what constitutes success and attractiveness. What you haven't been given much instruction about, however, is how to develop and utilize the Center of Your Head.

The clarity of the Center of Your Head affects the health and quality of your life experience as much as your brain and body does. This is where we go to solve problems, daydream and simply listen. When the Center of Your Head is clean and quiet, you're ready to begin creating with full potential. Have you ever felt the creative urge to cook something delicious and then walked into the kitchen to find it littered with dishes and towels and remnants of meals past? In your enthusiasm for the new project, you probably took time to prepare the space, wipe the counters and clean the kitchen before preparing the dish. In order to enjoy the preparation phase your special meal, it's necessary to clean up and make the kitchen ready. It's not comfortable to chop vegetables when the counters are piled high. You remove old clutter and energy and re-set the room for your purpose.

The same is true for the Center of Your Head. When you attempt to make decisions, solve problems or design something delicious while sitting in a place that is cluttered and dusty or filled with other people's opinions, you can get confused and lose your motivation or creativity. Before you can be an effective creator and a Master Thinker, you must first clean the Center of Your Head and make it yours.

Energy Tool #2
Center of Your Head

1. Find a quiet place to sit where you won't be disturbed for a few minutes. Your office, with door closed, can work.

2. Get comfortable and check in with your Grounding Line. If using your Grounding Line has become a part of your life, you will find it is virtually always attached.

3. When you first begin identifying the Center of Your Head, you may need to use your fingers (remember this is kindergarten. Besides, no one is watching you right now anyway). Close your eyes and place the index finger of each hand above and slightly to the front of each ear. Draw an imaginary line between your fingertips.

4. Now, move one index finger to a point in the center of your forehead and the other directly behind your head. Draw another imaginary line.

5. Notice where the two lines intersect. This is the exact location of the Center of Your Head.

6. Take a breath and begin to create a room at the intersection of the two lines. It can be a place in nature or a room with walls. Imagine this place with any décor you'd like. Include the hot tub and ultimate sound system if you wish or the babbling creek and redwood trees. Make it yours. Own it. Take your time and give yourself permission to imagine.

7. Visualize a comfortable chair or bed or place to stand in the Center of Your Head. This will be "Command Central," and from here you will direct creations, decisions and solutions. Some people enjoy installing a control panel with dials and switches.

8. Look around. If you find any living creature in there with you, be it human or animal, ask them to leave, return to the center of their heads, or stand outside the boundaries of your space. This is your turf and your time – alone. When others are in the Center of Your Head, they tend to give their opinions and influence your decisions and creations. This is the pattern you are changing. You may enjoy making an amusing trap door to dispose of stubborn visitors. Or create various enticements to move them outside. Whatever works, use it.

When you are comfortable in there, and the kitchen counters are clean, you may begin cooking (so to speak). Here are some ideas for experimentation:

• Experiment with noticing your Grounding Line from the Center of Your Head.

• Notice the sounds and sensations around your physical body. Notice if you can keep your attention in the Center of Your Head or if your attention moves to the sound. You can't get this wrong either way.

• Notice what thoughts or people, concerns or noise begin to pop up. Sometimes as we begin to take management of our attention and intentionally direct it to what interests us, the old thoughts and people we've been giving attention to all these years may protest by appearing or voicing their opinions. Begin to intentionally throw these noisy people down the Line.

• How does your body feel? You may notice new sensations such as tingling and warmth.

• You may add to and subtract from the décor as your mood and needs change.

As you practice sitting in the Center of Your Head, you will experience a stillness and ebbing away of stress and noise. Balance returns to your mind and body and emotions. This is a place of power, for when you are still and balanced, with your attention focused and uncluttered, decisions are sharper, creations are fuller and solutions are clearer. Making business and life decisions while sitting comfortably in the Center of Your Head will be stress-free and accurate.

▲

Chapter Four
Hello, Should, No, I

Argue for your limitations, and sure enough, they're yours.
Richard Bach, Illusions

Words are an easy and convenient place to observe our patterns of belief. Words are the physical representation of our thought patterns and a major part of our environment. What we believe, we say. What we say, we feel. And what we feel, say and believe, we then act upon. How we act is how we experience life. Whether a thought pattern is helping you or hindering you, simply noticing words indicative of the pattern will assist in altering and even repatterning that habit of thought. You may begin by noticing the words other people use. I suspect you'll soon discover that the unhappiest people you know are always talking about how rotten life is and how poorly they've been treated. The most satisfied and prosperous people you know will be talking about how great and miraculous their life experience is. Funny how that works.

The Law of Likes

The Law of Likes states, "Like attracts like." Birds of a feather – you know the cliche's. Abraham-Hicks calls it the Law of Attraction (3). The same principle is also referred to as the Law of Resonance. Where you put your attention (thought) is what you draw into your experience. Here is how it works: Next time you are waiting in a line, listen to the conversations around you and notice if people talk about how bad it is. "It" could be anything: the weather, the long line, their joints, their last hair cut, their doctor, ulcers, job, wife, kids, husband. People often enjoy congregating and complaining about "Ain't it awful." In doing so, they perpetuate their condition. They are repeating their thoughts over and over, attracting like-minded people into their vortex of pain and making their pain very real. As this pain is made more and more dominant in their thoughts and lives, eventually that's all they experience. Pain.

●●●

Recently I attended a celebration at a student's home for an important job he successfully completed. As I wandered around, I stopped at a particularly interesting conversation. A man was telling another about his physical aches and pains in great detail. The listener was very empathic and even moved his body closer to the speaker to better engage with him, and share his own diseases. There happened to be one ailment the listener didn't have that the speaker was describing in explicit detail. When he finished hearing the story of woe, the listener said, with a look of disappointment, "Oh, I don't have that illness, yet." Yet! Well, if he continues to think and talk the way he was demonstrating at the party, it certainly won't be long until he does. He received, with great openness and eagerness, enough details of the illness that if a minor symptom ever did appear, it could be easily labeled as the ailment itself!

•••

You may have also experienced the reverse of the above "Ain't it awful" syndrome. This one occurs much more rarely than the first. You see, "Ain't it awful" is culturally supported and considered politically correct. Entire industries depend upon it. Imagine someone in your office walking around through all the departments talking about how great they feel today and how they have an abundance of money, are going on a super vacation to the islands and how they just had a great work-out and lost ten pounds. In a very short period of time, this person would have no friends and would be the subject of gossip. It just isn't acceptable to talk about how great life is, but if you watch the very few who do, you'll notice one very important thing about them. They are happy and healthy, vibrant and joyful. My suggestion? Be on the lookout for these rare birds. Snap their picture in your mind's eye and begin to do what they do…that is if you also wish to be happy and healthy, vibrant and joyful. Otherwise, I'll give you the telephone number of the doctor's office where that party-goer frequents. I'm sure you'll meet him very shortly. He's the 50-year-old who looks to be 100.

So, if you are desiring to adjust that bottom building block of thought, in order to make your culture the way that pleases you, begin by listening to others and what they talk about. Be a scientist and notice how what they are saying (and therefore believing) is impacting their bodies, minds and emotions. You might also begin to pay attention to some of the words you discover falling out of your mouth. Here are a few words that have a powerful effect upon how we experience life.

Hello

The most positively powerful, least understood and seldom used word today is "Hello." "Hello" influences everyone and everything. Have you ever walked down the street and said "Hello" to someone? It is literally impossible for them to ignore this powerful and direct word. Even if they turn away uncomfortably, they have been affected. Perhaps you've even had that experience yourself. When you send a "Hello" to another person, it is as though you are directing a bright light onto them. They are seen. "Hello. I see you."

And then they either shine under that glow or turn from it. They may shine back at you and return the "Hello" or they may turn away uncomfortably. Why do they turn away? Why have you? People turn away from "Hello" because there is an internal pain that causes them to hide. When the light of "Hello" is shined upon you, all your beauty and inner strength is lit up. If you do not believe this truth about yourself or if you are not aligned with that inner strength, then the light of "Hello" only draws attention to the imbalance and that contrast feels uncomfortable.

•••

Jason, a junior high school student, has experimented with this potent word. Because he is so capable and bright, many of the other students couldn't relate to him and he felt friendless and socially awkward. For three days, Jason agreed to look at the face of every student he passed, (not necessarily the eyes) and say "Hello." That's all - no conversation, just "Hello." Not only did he have fun, but by the end of the three days, students were saying "Hello" to him, inviting him to parties and a girl even telephoned him!

•••

Ever notice what happens when you say "Hello" to young children? They shine right back at you. It's not necessary to say it out loud to a child. They will hear it and be affected by it anyway. One day I experimented with a child on an airplane. I silently began with "Hello," sent from the Center of My Head. I then proceeded to communicate with the child about the food (he loved strawberries), the landscape below, the last time he flew (without the use of an airplane, that is) and the experience of being in a small body. We laughed a great deal and had a good 90-minute flight. The child's mom was happily reading her novel, unaware of our interchange.

"Hello" (silent or spoken) affects all humans. It also affects animals, plants and body parts! Have you ever noticed what happens when you say "Hello" to a dog? I mean really say "Hello"– from your center? Most dogs (unless they've been beaten up) will turn inside-out to say "Hello" back to you!

Experiment with your dog

The results are more dramatic if Rover is in the same room with you.

1. Begin with your mind quiet and your emotions in a good feeling place. You can do this by sitting quietly for a few moments, using your Grounding Line and finding the Center of Your Head.

2. Think of your dog friend. Remember a time when you enjoyed physical contact with him.

3. Fully re-experience the event of wrestling around or romping with him. Allow the emotion to build up and fill your body and mind with this affection and play.

4. Look over at him and send all this good feeling into the Center of His Head. You might play with putting the scene in a bubble and floating it over into his head.

5. Really focus this attention silently at him.

6. When he responds, increase the intensity of the energy, while still remaining silent.

7. Try not to smile as you watch him try to wriggle out of his skin to say "Hello" back to you. Good luck.

8. Continue this for as long as you and he can stand it. You may

find the response surprising and heart warming.

The more you allow this energy to build up in your space before you flow it onto your canine friend, the greater his response. Warning: This experiment may cause a new level of bonding between the two of you that escalates as you play with this tool. This telepathic communication of Spirit to Spirit extends beyond time and space.

Cats respond to "Hello" slightly differently than dogs. Cats think they invented telepathy, so their response to "Hello" may be more subtle. We live with an extremely telepathic cat and we communicate frequently.

Try this experiment with your cat

You may enjoy the results more if Puff (?!) is not in the same room with you, but in another part of the house.

1. Begin with a quiet mind and your emotions, positive.

2. Ground and be in the Center of Your Head. Closing your eyes is helpful.

3. Think of your cat friend. Pretend you see the top of her head and just pretend it is a color. Make it up. Go with the first color you get.

4. Make the top of your head this identical color. You may even imagine a line of this color running between the tops of your heads.

5. Remember a time when you enjoyed cuddling and scratching her ears and nuzzling with her affectionately.

6. Really re-experience this memory. Allow the emotion to build up and fill your body and mind with this energy.

7. Visualize sending this good feeling picture across the line of color and into the Center of Her Head. Really focus this attention silently at her and pour it into her head.

8. Allow the memory and emotion to continue and increase.

9. Remain silent and smile. Let it feel good to *you*.

10. Continue this outpouring as you hear her purr or feel her jump upon your lap.

I use this tool when "Bel" is outdoors and I want her to return. It takes only a few minutes of this focused work before she appears. I also use it while presenting seminars out of town. A long distance "Hello" keeps her happy. When I return home, she greets me with affection now, rather than with disdain.

"Hello" sent to a body part is the major component to bringing the body back to alignment. When you send "Hello (I see you)" to a body part, that part lights up and says "Hello" back, just like the dog or child. When you say "Hello" to a body part that is out of balance, it begins to return to balance. "Hello, I see you" is more than simple words. Underlying those words is the energy, "Hello, I see how great you are." A body part will respond to those words (and the intentional energy behind them) just as a child or animal will. That body part, when given a sincere "Hello," will begin to align itself to show you how great it really is. Like the dog, it will begin to turn inside-out to show you how much health and vitality, appreciation and gratitude it contains.

Pretend you're a scientist and see what happens when you begin to intentionally add this magic word to your life. Did you see the movie *Patch Adams*? Robin Williams conducted a "Hello Experiment." He timed and recorded the number of seconds it took for people on the street to return the "Hello" he sent. Soon he met an elderly woman who looked quite fearful of this crazed man. Patch said "Hello" and the woman responded with a frown and walked past him. He continued to time the event until she stopped a few steps away and turned back toward him with a big, wide, beaming smile. He simply laughed and recorded the time. (4)

"Hello" works no matter what. Experiment and notice how it changes your life. Like Jason, perhaps you could begin to say, "Hello (I see how great you are)" to people you pass at school or at work. Watch what happens. You may find dogs follow you around, or better yet, a girl might telephone you!

Should

As you observe the words others use, soon you will discover certain words falling out of your mouth that don't feel good or don't support the prosperity and well-being you really desire. One word that is most revealing is the word "Should." This word (and its derivatives and substitutes) indicates where programming lies. A "Should" is used to convince someone else to, "Do it my way. My way is the best way."

Notice how frequently adults use "Should" on children. You may also notice how you "Should" on others and "Should" on yourself. We all have done it. We don't use "Should" to intentionally hurt another person. We just want them to behave more like us and therefore make us more comfortable. This underlying desire however, can deeply limit the self-esteem and creative growth of children. "Should" prevents them from discovering their own passion. Some of us "Should" quite often. Shoulding on each other; Shoulding on the kids; Shoulding on ourselves. What a mess. "Should" all over the place!

●●●

I was married to a Marine for many years. After the marriage dissolved and we moved on, I was packing clothes one night for a business trip. I packed and unpacked several times, never getting it quite right. I folded the clothes then unfolded them, rolled the clothes then unrolled them, then folded them again. It was getting late. I was getting tired and frustrated. What was going on? Why was it so difficult to complete this simple task? I finally surrendered, sat down on the edge of the bed and began to use my Energy Tools to Ground and find the Center of My Head. Almost immediately I heard my ex-husband telling me. "You *should* always roll your clothes just like this whenever you pack!" What a surprise; my ex was still Shoulding on me after all these years and influencing my ability to pack a suitcase! I laughed at myself, did some quick energy work to release that bit of programming, quickly packed my suitcase and went to bed. I've been able to pack suitcases ever since.

No

As children begin to notice and establish the distinction between themselves and others, they learn the word "No." Two-year-olds use it profusely as a way to define their identity, unique from others. They don't say "No" to be mean or obstinate or ugly, as you probably notice if you're around children. Two-year-olds use this word simply to define their boundaries. They also use words such as "Mine" for the same purpose – to identify themselves as separate from everyone else.

As you become a healthy adult you develop a strong sense of self and what works for you. You learn to identify yourself as a separate entity from workmates, lovers and acquaintances. The word "No" is no longer used to mark the difference between you and others. It is used to communicate a desire or preference. Sometimes, in not-so-healthy adults, "No" is still used to establish boundaries that are not strongly in place or are shaky and unsure. I've noticed that women do this more often than men. This is because, generally, women have not been given the permission and safety in this culture to establish natural, strong boundaries. Nor do most women know the difference between themselves and others. Women have been trained to be givers and healers of others and have learned to put everyone else's needs before their own. The response of "No" gives the woman the necessary time to think the question over and come up with the true response. Unfortunately for her, once "No" is pronounced, life continues on that basis and by the time she has decided what she really wants, the opportunity has passed. She can always say "No" later, when she has more information. Try beginning from "Yes" or "Maybe" instead of "No" and watch what happens.

A variation of "No" is simply to view a question or opportunity from an attitude of limitation. "What are the ways this will not work?" is "No" worded slightly differently.

•••

Uncle Walter is an extremely creative man. He has had new ideas and projects bubbling abundantly in his life for as long as I can remember. His half-completed art projects, income ideas or attempts at carpentry were always a part of my life. In fact, sometimes I think that is why Walter moved to the country, so he could build as many workshops as he desired. Walter finally stopped at four. This ability to create in unlimited ways always delighted me and gave me permission to embrace my own version of creative passion.

Just as there is a yin to a yang, Uncle Walter is married to a woman who is also quite creative in her own right. Her creativity is practical, purposeful and utilitarian, however. If it doesn't have an immediate and necessary use, it is not worth making. Her style of creating is quite different from Walter's style of, "Just slap it all together, trust the genius within and see what comes out. If we can use it for something later, great, if not, just enjoy the heck out of nailing it all up." Because of their differing styles, Marge and Walter never work on projects together. Walter dreams of co-creating with a partner and always enthusiastically invites his wife to join him. When Marge does try to work with him, she brings along "No." In other words, she begins the project with limitations. "What could go wrong with this idea? Has it already been done? Will it make us any money? How much is it going to cost us this time?" Invariably, before the project can fly, it is shot down with "No's." Marge and Walter are in their 70's now and maintain their separate creative lives, never fully partnering to fly together.

I

How do these phrases make you feel?

I'm just hanging in there.	I need a vacation.
I'll try.	I don't know.
I can't.	I don't feel so hot.
How can I be so dumb?	I really screwed up
I can do this.	Yeah! I did it.
I feel great.	How can I make this work?
I like what I did here.	I like me.

"I" is a call for a wish to be granted. Any word (and therefore thought and belief) that follows "I" is what you are asking for. You are setting in motion the creative process toward that thing following "I." The choice is yours. Do you desire just hanging in there or feeling great? Are you asking for examples of how you are dumb or how you are successful? If we hold the premise that our thoughts create our feelings and our feelings create our experience, what experience are you asking for? Only you can think your thoughts, feel your feelings and live your life. Misery IS optional.

Chapter Five

NITs into PITs

Becoming Aware is 96% of the game of change. The next 3% is getting Amused at what you just became Aware of. If you can become Amused at what you just became Aware of, then the last 1% is easy — just choose to do something a little different.

Have you ever had the experience of innocently going about your day and suddenly noticing a negative thought "out of nowhere" appearing in your mind that has nothing to do with the circumstance at hand? An entire story unfolds, much to your surprise, a story that you didn't consciously create? Have you ever walked down the street, observed a person you didn't know and found a series of thoughts pop into your mind that were negative assumptions about them? You might find yourself experiencing a judgment about the type of person they are or about their habits.

This occurs quite frequently when we observe a person of extreme physical proportions, either very thin or very heavy in weight. The next time you are out in a crowd of people, you might experiment by noticing the unsolicited thoughts and judgments that appear in your consciousness about others around you. These assumptions are many times based upon group agreements and cultural beliefs about the appearance of that person. For example, observing a large bodied woman, one might have the automatic assumption that she is lazy and eats too much, and engages in very little physical exercise. When we observe a woman who is very thin in stature, we might have the automatic thought that she is anorexic. When we observe a woman with a tight little body, we might assume she is healthy and works out or that she knows she is attractive and is snobbish.

We also have these Negative Intrusive Thoughts (NITs) about ourselves. Have you ever looked in the mirror and automatically had the thought pop into your head about something that doesn't look *right*? "My eyes are crooked." "These fat thighs are disgusting." You might also find your mind revealing NITs pertaining to your emotional and mental states as well. "Man, you're such a dependent cry baby." "Gosh, will I ever get this right?" "How could I have been so stupid?" These Negative Intrusive Thoughts indicate a deeper, well-established, unsupportive belief system.

Until you are conscious of these Negative Intrusive Thoughts, you are at the mercy of the outer world's values, conditions and beliefs. These NITs are not truly what you believe as a spiritual being. They are simply the rocks that you lazily picked up along the hiking trail of life and dropped into your backpack. Some of us have picked up so many of these rocks that we walk with shoulders bent, minds clouded and emotions out of whack due to the heavy weight of beliefs we carry around.

The trick to emptying your backpack of these rocks, or NITs, is to become aware of them. The quickest way out of the mud is to first recognize you're in it. By simply noticing the NITs and the false beliefs backing them up, we begin to let go of them.

Negative Intrusive Thoughts have created a neuro-pathway in your brain that is continually reinforced and strengthened, each time you participate in that habit of thought, until there exists a wide, six lane, concrete super-highway between your thoughts and resulting experiences. And this is a highway that you automatically enter everyday, without even questioning it, or noticing it. As you become aware of (with amusement) the NITs in your head, the highway begins to crack and disintegrate. Great. Eventually, the road must be repaired. That's where the PITs, Positive Intentional Thoughts, come in. You are intentionally re-patterning or re-programming your thoughts for your personal benefit and well-being, rather than continuing to be dragged around by the NITs and the results they create. Your life experience immediately changes.

How to change NITs into PITs

First you must make the personal commitment to do *whatever it takes* to experience greater success and happiness in life. Then you must embrace the necessary ingredients of amusement and curiosity. Remember that you are the scientist studying your own life. When you do, the process becomes easier and the changes begin to unfold, almost effortlessly. When you simply have the *intention* to become more aware of these patterns, they begin to reveal themselves automatically, sometimes quite loudly, consistently and unavoidably. If you don't choose to look, no problem, the pattern will scream louder. Still too busy to look? No problem. It will soon get really loud until you can't ignore it. Do you know others who ignore the oh-so-obvious (to you) destructive patterns in their lives until an event wakes them up and they must listen? Many people create crisis (health, mental, business, relationship) in order to bring their attention to what is crying out to be resolved.

Exercise

Now's your chance to don your magnifying glass and Sherlock Holmes pipe. Carry a small spiral notebook with you. This is your NIT to PIT catalog. As you move about your day, you will become aware of NITs. You will notice judgments and criticism, put-downs and intolerances toward yourself and others. Write them down. All of them. As you begin to do this, you may find your notebook out of your pocket more often than in your pocket. This is normal. As you continue with this exercise, it gets easier and you'll find fewer and fewer NITs passing through your mind. Write one NIT per page. Some NITs will resurface, again and again and again. You may simply make marks on the original page, indicating each return of the NIT. (Sounds like a cheap sci-fi movie doesn't it? "Return of the Killer NITs." It may feel that way too. Humorously so.)

> ### NIT into PIT Hint
> Sometimes beginning a new pattern is easier with a buddy. Find a PIT-Partner if you need some support. You'll both have more fun and the re-patterning process will be easier and faster.

Later, as you are waiting at the bank or the grocery store or at home relaxing, bring your NIT to PIT notebook out and slowly, with amusement and appreciation, thumb through the pages. Read each NIT and notice how many times it returned to your mind. With ease, choose one NIT and on that page, write a corresponding PIT. You are re-patterning the NIT here, so it is very important to take your time and have fun. You may even notice more NITs pass through as you do this exercise. It's okay, write them down. "This is a stupid exercise. Why did I ever say I was going to do this?" A corresponding PIT to the above NIT would be something like, "It's really important to me that I become aware of my Negative Intrusive Thoughts. I want to be in command of my life." Here are more examples:

NIT: Gosh, I'm fat.
    – PIT: I respect and love my body and its wisdom.

NIT: What is their problem? Why don't they wake up and move ahead in line?
    – PIT: This isn't a race. I enjoy every moment of my day.

NIT: I'm stuck and feel lousy.
    – PIT: This is just a Growth Period (See Chapter Eleven). This means I'm moving into something bigger and better.

NIT: How could I make such a dumb mistake?
    – PIT: Well that was an interesting way to solve that challenge. I'm sure something good will come of it.

NIT: She talks too much.
    – PIT: It's entertaining to watch how others live their lives.

NIT: He sure is a lazy bum.
    – PIT: He really knows how to enjoy his time. So do I.

NIT: This project is much too difficult for me.
    – PIT: How is it possible to make this fun and successful?

And the all time favorite PIT:

This is not a problem.

It's only energy.

It's only energy.

It's only energy.

▲

Chapter Six

Spinning Wheels

The man who has no imagination has no wings.

Mohammad Ali

Every thing, every animal, every smell, every insect, rock, chair, element, thought, person, color, sound, taste, emotion, sensation and word is energy. Everything is energy and everything is vibrating at its own unique rate.

There are many energy centers or vortexes in your body. These energy centers go by the common name of *chakras*. Chakras mechanically increase or decrease the energy that flows through your body's channels, much like transformers adjust the flow of electricity through machines. When open and allowing the flow, a chakra is approximately one and one-half inch in diameter. When it is decreasing the flow, it is approximately one inch wide. Open isn't necessarily "good" and closed isn't "bad." The degree to which the chakra is open is the degree to which it is in use at the moment. Here is an example:

Your first chakra's job is to keep the body safe. When safety or survival is threatened, this energy center opens up and tells the rest of the system to wake up, turn on and take care of the emergency. You've probably heard stories of ordinary people who find themselves in life threatening situations and automatically summon super-human strength to rip off car doors, lift heavy equipment or sprint at lightening speed. In such times a person's first chakra opens up and sends alert signals that stimulate the muscles, glands, nerves, heart and mind to jump into action.

Each chakra has a specific job and is related to or influences a gland in the endocrine system. Each chakra also holds one or more Spiritual Ability. By that I mean the abilities your Spiritual Self knows all about and can exercise if allowed. These include such abilities as telepathy, clairvoyance, affinity, clairsentience, precognition and clairaudience. These abilities naturally came with the body and they haven't been allowed to grow and develop in most of us. The following chart explains in greater detail the major eleven chakras (seven within the body and four within the hands and feet) and their associated glands and Spiritual Abilities.

As you become more familiar with your own energy centers, your understanding and Truth may or may not resonate with this information. Please use this only as a beginning guide and trust your own intuition.

Energy Centers:

Chakra	Location	Endocrine Gland	Job and Ability
1st	Lowest tip of spine	Adrenals	-Keeps your body safe
2nd	Two fingers below navel	Ovaries/ Testes	-Emotions -Sexuality -Clairsentience -Male/female creativity
3rd	Solar Plexus	Pancreas	-Ability to operate your body - Ability to have and remember dreams*
4th	Center of the chest	Thymus	-Affinity with Self & world
5th	Throat	Thyroid	-Communication -Clairaudience - Inner voice -Common Sense -Telepathy
6th	Forehead just above eyes	Pituitary	-Clairvoyance - Spacial awareness
7th	Soft spot of skull	Pineal	-Knowing your own truth -Precognition
Hands	Tenderest spot of palm		-Creativity & healing
Feet	Tenderest spot of arch		-Relationship to Earth

The Third Chakra is also where we hold beliefs pertaining to judgment, power, control and resistance.

▲

Chapter Seven

Burr Creek

Meditation is very much like training a puppy. You put the puppy down and say, "Stay." Does the puppy listen? It gets up and runs away. You sit the puppy back down again, "Stay." And the puppy runs away over and over again. Sometimes the puppy jumps up, runs over, and pees in the corner. Our minds are much the same as the puppy, only they create even bigger messes. In training the mind, or the puppy, we have to start over and over again.
          Jack Kornfield, A Path With Heart

I did most of my growing up in a small town in Michigan. In 1968, my parents moved three daughters, two cats and a Chihuahua from Detroit to 130 acres of meadows and woods, lake and creek, house, barns and garden plots. The creek was named Burr.

 Burr Creek was spring fed and icy cold. In the summer months, beavers slowed the prolific flow with their twig tunnels and wooden homes. It was their way of life and they probably would have called it "fun." In the winter months neighbors slowed the flow of Burr Creek by violently, deeply, criss-crossing their snowmobiles through it. That was their way of life and they also called it fun. Every year, both beavers and men would take nature into their hands (or paws) and change her to suit their needs or whims.

Burr Creek never really minded much. Any torn and woven logs, tumbled or jammed rocks, stray sticks or pebbles would soon be quickly moved aside by the current of her narrow, rushing waters. Nothing that man nor beaver put in her way would last long through her incessant pounding and pushing, her continuous movement and flow. Eventually and predictably, Burr would take seniority again and move out the debris that didn't belong to her, dump it into the lake and out into who-knows-where. We never really cared where. It was gone and the creek flowed free again. The trout returned every year, as did the deer and raccoon, mallards and herons. Moss grew thick and the woodland wildflowers densely flourished again as Burr fed them her life force. Every year. Just as regular and predictable as beavers and men.

Burr Creek flows through your body. You have narrow, prolifically flowing channels of life continuously moving like creeks, through their specific paths. Just like Burr, logs and rocks occasionally block the flow of Life Force, but the pulse continues and soon your flow of energy returns to well-being. Just like the creek. The logs and pebbles in your creeks are the limiting beliefs and patterns that are keeping you from fully pumping that Life Force through your body and through your life. Your external culture, whether that be family, religion, country or business, convinced you to embrace their rules and way of living. What did you know? You were just a small child and they were bigger and older and "wiser." You agreed to play, however those rules never quite sat well in your body, mind and emotions. Your spirit grew to feel cramped and inhibited. What began as a small belief, compounded and reinforced, became a large, roadblock in your life. For example, a belief picked up in first grade about your slowness to learn, may now affect your ability to get a good job. That belief is simply a rock in your creek and it is keeping your natural Certainty and abundance from flowing. Patterns that have been lodged in your life and creek for a long time are pretty well jammed in there. And the longer they've been there, or the stronger the emotional charge around them, the more likely they will be affecting you physically, emotionally and mentally. Those patterns are not problems. They are simply energy in the form of logs and rocks that have been in your creek and are now ready to be released. Evidence of this logjam is sometimes quite obvious and disruptive in your life.

●●●

When Marie was eight years old, her sister, Jo, was four. It was the usual hot and humid summer and they were at a store, descending an escalator with their mom. At the bottom of the escalator, Jo's flip-flop got caught in the prongs and was pulled off her foot. Her toe was cut by the prongs and was bleeding. Mom went into a panic. Her caring, maternal instinct turned on. The defense system of her body was alerted and was prepared to defend her brood at all costs. (Her first chakra also widened.) Suddenly she was filled with the fear that her two daughters would be sucked down that little crack. She yelled at Jo and Marie and told them how stupid and careless they were. She yelled at the store manager who had quickly come over to quiet her down. She told her young daughters how dangerous and deadly escalators are and how they should be banned. She had a great deal of strong emotion and a strong judgment. On that day, because she loved her daughters and wanted them to be forever safe, Mom gave them the powerful belief that escalators were deadly and should be avoided.

That was about 37 years ago. Jo still can't bring herself to step upon an escalator. In fact, she completely avoids every one of them and has consequently learned a great deal about the service halls and back stairs of major department stores. That short three minute experience when she was four was the log that jammed her Life Force and may forever cause her to fear escalators. It is simply a limiting belief that became stuck in her space because of a strong combination of emotion and judgment. She avoids that part of life.

Marie, on the other hand, used her Energy Tools and now confidently steps on escalators with no fear, even with her arms full, and dragging a suitcase.

Energy Tool #3
Flowing the River, Part One

1. Find a quiet place where you won't be disturbed for a few minutes. This tool is most affective when used first thing in the morning, before the responsibilities of the day demand your attention. During the day, take a moment at your desk.

2. Closing your eyes allows for better focus.

3. Sit comfortably with both feet flat on the floor.

4. Find the Center of Your Head and invite any noise or visitors to leave. Get comfortable there in your imaginary workshop, behind your eyes. Pretend you have a comfortable chair to sit in or a mossy rock.

5. Attach your Grounding Line and turn it on to magnetically release the noise. Do this for a few minutes before continuing.

6. With your imaginary hands, reach down deeply into the earth and pretend you are pulling up rich, nurturing, abundant Earth Energy.

7. Visualize this energy moving from deep within the earth up into your right foot chakra. You may imagine this flowing energy as a color if you like.

8. Visualize this flow of energy as it travels up the center of your leg, into your knee, across your thigh, into the tip of your spine and down your Grounding Line. Go as slowly as possible.

9. Notice how different your right leg feels from your left.

10. Repeat for your left leg. Proceed as slowly as possible.

Allow these two channels run for a short time and just notice what you notice. You may experience warmth, discomfort, coolness, tingling or nothing. There is no right or wrong way. We're just playing here. This is kindergarten, remember?

11. Remain there as long as possible. You may notice stray thoughts or images pop up. Just allow them to move out. As the pebbles and logs of limiting beliefs loosen and flow away, the memories connected to them are showing themselves to you. It's just energy, and as you continue to allow this flow, charged past events in your life will lose their strength and you will simply experience neutral memories. You may also experience the permission and freedom they were preventing.

12. When you're ready to begin your day, slowly move your toes and fingers; bend down toward the floor; open your eyes down there and slowly sit up, move around and stand.

I suspect you'll now notice feelings of greater stability, calm, ease and balance as you move about your day. Feel free to occasionally check in on the energy flowing through your leg channels. Putting your attention on them, lightly throughout the day, will keep the creeks flowing well.

•••

I first met Mark in a beginning class about three years ago. He was 45. As I walked the class through this Energy Tool, Mark began to fidget and couldn't sit still. After class he said his legs have ached for years and felt very stiff and uncomfortable during the visualization, especially his right knee. This disappointed and confused him and Mark wanted to quit our class, thinking he was a failure. I encouraged him to hang in there and just allow his river to continue to flow; eventually the log in his knee would wash away. He understood it was just energy that had been there a very long time. He always believed he wasn't coordinated or graceful. During the following week's class, Mark remembered an embarrassing time when this knee had "gone out" in college during a New Year's dance he'd attended. He hadn't really danced much before that night, or after, and had completely forgotten that event. What was really happening was Mark's limiting belief was jarred loose and bumping around a bit before it left for good.

He did continue and during the third week's class. Mark's legs stopped hurting and he discovered an old desire to move his body. Some vague memories of his childhood now made sense to him. From the moment he could walk, Mark was a dancer. He loved to surrender his mind and move his body to music. Any kind of music. As a very young child, he would close his eyes and sway and wiggle to songs on the radio, while his mother applauded and supported him. His dad, however had another opinion about boys who danced. Dad worked hard for his meager wage and believed any son of his should do the same. Mark loved his Dad and wanted to please him, so kept his dancing behind doors. When, at fifteen years old, Mark applied to attend a local summer dance troupe, Dad had a strong reaction, as you might guess, and refused to sign the registration. Mark evaluated the situation and decided it was more important to get the approval of his father. Besides, "You can't make money doing art." That summer he worked for a neighborhood landscaper, hauling dirt.

That early invalidation stayed in Mark's legs and built up to a painful crescendo. It was finally released when he allowed Life Force to pulse through his channels. Every physical ailment has a non-physical counterpart. Mark didn't have to understand it logically for it to clear. He just deliberately moved his attention to his energy channels and like Burr Creek, Mark's limiting beliefs, patterns, pebbles and logs were jarred loose and released from his experience.

Energy Tool #4
Flowing the River, Part Two

This is the sister of the tool above and is best used during the same session and after you get your leg channels running.

1. Still sitting comfortably in the Center of Your Head, reach up above your head into the heights of the atmosphere with your imaginary hands (or with your physical hands if you like). Pull into the top of your head great amounts of brilliant Universal Life Force Energy. You can imagine this as a color or texture, water or light. By the way, this works even if you notice nothing.

2. Visualize it flowing down the back of your head, splitting at the base of your neck and running down both sides of your spine.

3. Allow a bit of it to flow down your Grounding Line.

4. The rest of this energy will continue to turn and flow upward, on each side of the chakras. It will do this effortlessly. Your body was designed for this work and has the inner wisdom and memory of it.

5. Watch from the Center of Your Head as this flow of energy grabs a bit of the Earth Energy on its way up, for balance.

6. Allow this energy mix to fountain out the top of your head and spill out all around you, within your energy field.

7. Some of this energy mix will now take a detour at your throat and run down both arms and out your hand chakras.

8. Take a breath. Allow this flow to continue as long as possible. In a very short period of time, you will be able to notice the leg, back, front and arm channels all flowing like creeks, as you sit in the Center of Your Head.

It usually takes between 20 and 40 minutes to completely move all the noise out of your space – from the loudest voices to the subtlest whispers. If you can make the time to allow your rivers of energy to continue to flow through your channels for an hour or more, you'll experience greater benefit and more complete clearing of the logjams. I suspect you will also now experience still greater levels of calm and centeredness, ease and quiet. With very little effort, your mind will become still and your body, aligned and balanced.

•••

Ted has been a successful computer programmer in the San Francisco Bay Area for many years. He works on a contract basis, from his home. Occasionally he must go into a company's facility to complete a project or coordinate with others there. He also instructs employees on the operation of newly designed programs or systems. When Ted is working alone, all is well. He's happy and efficient, creative and satisfied. When he interfaces with others, Ted notices his hands and feet sweat profusely and his throat swells up to such a degree, he can barely croak out explanations. At these moments, he is struck with fear, not only of speaking, but that these other professionals will notice and judge his disability.

Ted knew this was just energy connected to an old belief pattern that he was stupid. You see, Ted's dad was a successful, published scientist with a well-developed analyzer. Since childhood, Ted always struggled to please his father intellectually and always seemed to fail. He never quite measured up to his father's standard. His father called him slow and stupid. Ted was neither. Knowing this was the pattern, however, didn't make it any easier to live with. This stupid-belief was so ingrained in Ted's body the reaction of suffocation and sweating would occur automatically. Ted's physical manifestation had a non-physical component (stupid-belief) that was ready to be released.

Over a period of several months, as Ted ran this energy down the channels in his throat, neck, arms and hands, the anxiety and worry ceased. He released the stuck energy and stupid-belief and replaced it with Certainty. The sweating and croaking seldom occurs these days.

Energy Tool #5
Replenishing Tool

After you have spent as long as possible clearing out your creeks and rivers, it's a good idea to replenish those areas that are now open and clear. You have emptied your channels of stale, unbeneficial energy and beliefs, and now it is time to fill them up with energy and beliefs that are matched to you in present-time.

1.   Visualize a large ball of Golden Light about a foot above your head. This ball of light contains all of your essence as a spirit, without the baggage you've collected in life. It contains who you really are as the greater, wiser, bigger, purer part of you. The you as Spirit.

2.   This Golden Ball also contains any positive aspect you assign to it such as Gratitude, Appreciation, Trust, Permission, Certainty, Presence, and Joy. This would be an excellent opportunity to re-pattern any NITs you may have moved out with a specific PIT in your Gold Ball.

3.   Give the command to the Gold Ball to attract this one positive aspect or PIT. Watch as it enlarges and brightens.

4.   Instruct the Gold Ball to magnetically attract to it any of your thoughts and attention you might have left other places throughout your day. Call your energy and attention back from work, relationship, the checkbook, etc.

5.   When you have an image of this Golden Ball above your head and it appears fully enlarged and bright, simply invite it to enter the top of your head and fill every cell of your body. Each cell will entrain to or match this new, fresh energy and return to balance. Each cell will fill up with the greater part of you and further release any of the pebbles or logs that have been stored there.

6.   Allow this Golden Light to travel down and fill every cell of your body, your Grounding Line and out to the edge of your electromagnetic field (a two-foot radius around your body.)

7. When you feel completely filled up and refreshed, simply bend over and stretch, or open your eyes and slowly begin your day.

Cellular biologist, Dr. Bruce Lipton (University of Wisconsin and Stanford University) has done extensive research on the effect thought has on the structure and health of cells.

Your cells see what you see. Cells are like cameras. Cells take what is in the environment and create a physical representation of it. For example, over 90% of cancers are not genetic or hereditary, but are the results of the individual's response to the environment. Therefore, if you change your belief about the environment, you can also change the cancer. Your perception or beliefs actually change your gene structure. In fact, your beliefs are running your entire biological system. (5)

Knowing this, wouldn't it make a whole lot of sense to fill those cells with Golden Light activated with Positive Intentional Thoughts?

Flowing Energy Diagram

Because Divine Energy is inherent in our biological system, every thought that crosses our minds, every belief we nurture, every memory to which we cling, translates into a positive or negative command to our bodies and spirits.
Carolyn Myss, Ph.D., Anatomy of the Spirit

▲

Chapter Eight
Office Babble

Rejoice in all your relationships, the ones that are easy and the ones that are not. They are bringing you exactly what you need to know for your soul's awakening and evolution.

Mary Manin Morrissey

I f you work in an office or among others, you may have noticed that there are some people who stand a little too close to you and make you feel physically uncomfortable. They "get in your face." Perhaps there are others in your life who continually bring their problems to you. Often while you are listening to them, you begin to feel tired and actually yawn. Then there are times when, after a wonderfully healing and uplifting conversation with you, your friend walks away feeling great, yet you feel spent. What has happened is this: You've matched your friend and some of her energy oozed over into your field while you allowed a portion of your own energy to be carried away by her.

You might look at it this way: Every living being and inanimate object is energy, vibrating at its own unique frequency. Your energy is unique and quite different from your friend's energy. Let's say your healthy, whole vibratory color is yellow and your friend's is red. As you talk to him and listen to his problems, his red comes over and meshes with your yellow, to create an orange. At the same time, some of your yellow has mingled with his red. Neither of you are as you were. You're both orange instead of your true color. Both of you have lost your integrity to become who you are not. You might begin to feel tired or irritated, distracted and spacey. That is the result of you mixing your energy with his. Wouldn't it be great to be a loving, compassionate friend and maintain your energetic integrity? Of course. While your energies are mixing and mingling, another thing is happening. Your friend's dramas and problems have also moved over into your energy field. Now, not only are you orange, you're getting sad and angry. And it wasn't even your drama to begin with!

During my corporate life, I interfaced with a full range of office characters including product designers, engineers, customer service reps, sales and marketing teams, even the stray accountant and controller. There was one character in this play who frequently affected me and even turned me a bit orange. Leena was the executive assistant who seemed to daily find her way into my office to "share" all the woes of her job, her boss and everyone else she knew. In explicit detail. Perhaps you know someone like this? Perhaps you even work with someone like this? Leena complained about everything and everyone. Her whole life was miserable and it was everyone else's fault. They were doing it to her and she was the innocent victim. I listened politely and tried to solve her problems. I listened politely and stopped my work. I listened politely and tried to heal her troubled life. An interesting observation: Leena continued to have the same problems over and over again, no matter what I sympathetically or empathetically suggested.

The Difference Between Empathy, Sympathy and Compassion

There is an important distinction between empathy and sympathy and compassion. When the beautiful bride falls into the deep end of the swimming pool, she completely soaks her gown and ruins her hair. Empathy is when you jump into the pool, fully dressed, and try to save her. As you know, drowning people tend to struggle and drag the rescuer down with them. And as Empathizer, that's exactly what happens – you get all wet and nearly drown. In this same situation, the Sympathizer wades into the water, neck deep, to reach as far as his arms will stretch in the attempt to save the beautiful, splashing, angry, bride. The result? Sympathizer is not successful at all, just really wet and tired.

As Compassionate Rescuer, you simply sit at the edge of the swimming pool with a long pole and offer it to the now, not-so-beautiful, bride. "Oh, I see you're in a really unfortunate predicament. What do you think would be the best way for you to change this? Here is a strong stick, if you are interested in using it." You don't get wet and she has the empowering experience of solving her own problem and pulling herself out of the drink. Empathizer and Sympathizer may be forcing assistance and advice onto the bride that she may not be willing, able or ready to accept. The Compassionate One gives her a choice and the tool to help herself. Such a compassionate hand may completely change the bride's life to one of greater Personal Power.

•••

When I first discovered the following tool in my toolbox, I practiced it on Leena. It immediately disrupted our pattern of communicating in a very gentle, unintrusive way. In fact what happened was, approximately a week later I heard her voice from a distant office. She was demonstrating the same behavior she used to exhibit in my office. This shift occurred so organically and easily, I hadn't even noticed she wasn't visiting me until many days had passed. Leena and I remained as friendly as ever and she never noticed the shift in our conversations. Our communication pattern was broken and Leena comfortably shifted her attention to someone else who didn't have this tool and was willing to continue with the pattern. So be it. I got a lot more work accomplished, more joyfully and with greater ease. She continued to get her needs met as well, by someone else, more sympathetic, down the hall in Customer Service. It is always win-win for everyone.

•••

This tool disrupts uncomfortable communication patterns between anyone, even between animals and humans. I've observed parents and children using it, marriage partners and business associates. It works. If you have ever found yourself repeating an identical argument with your partner, this simple tool may indeed help disrupt that communication pattern. Then the two of you can return to a more neutral state of being, for clearer discussion of the underlying issues.

Energy Tool #6
The Rose

Before beginning, determine what image you'd like to use for this Energy Tool. This image must be easy for you to picture, must have no negative charge for you and must include an attachment to the earth, similar to a Grounding Line. Most people use a rose. A rose fits all the criteria. It is easy to visualize, has no negative charge and has a natural Grounding Line (stem). A rose has also been used for this purpose for a very long time and there is a morphogenic field around it. Simply put, because this symbol has been used for this specific purpose by many practitioners and for many years, an energy vortex surrounds it that makes it much easier for beginners to use successfully. (6)

Although the Rose is well programmed for this type of work, feel free to create an object that works best for you. A florist friend of mine has a difficult time remaining neutral around roses and therefore uses a wild daisy for this tool. There is no right or wrong way. You can't make a mistake. The important point, however, is to decide what image you will use and continue to use it. Avoid switching and changing your mind. Doing so will cause the tool to lose its effectiveness. If you choose to use a rose, its color, openness and size doesn't influence its ability to do its job. A stem is important for grounding.

Okay, here's the tool:

1. Imagine or remember what a Rose looks like. Any color and shape will do.

2. Visualize placing your Rose on the edge of your energy field (approximately 18 inches to two feet) or half the distance between you and the other person, whichever is closest to your body.

3. If the other person moves toward you simply continue to move the Rose halfway between you and him, or her.

4. Stay on your side of the Rose. This means keeping all your energy and attention on your side. When you do, the other person will stay on their side of the Rose. You will be able to have a perfectly normal conversation with this person, as you talk through the Rose and simply allow it to do its job.

If your friend becomes emotional, or dramatic, the Rose will prevent her drama and pain from entering your field. In other words, your yellow and her red will maintain integrity.

Checking in with the Rose, cleaning it off or freshening it up occasionally is a good idea. Your casual attention to the Rose will refocus your awareness, strengthen your boundaries and rejuvenate the Rose's ability to disrupt communication patterns. Employing any effort to focus on it lessens its affectiveness. Remember, this is kindergarten. Results are greater if you remain at ease.

You will discover that by staying on your side of the Rose, you will experience a new feeling of neutrality. You can trust that your friend will be able to figure out her own problem and there is really nothing you can do to help her, except listen. And your friend really only wants someone to listen to her, with compassion. It's not your problem to solve. In fact, it is impossible for you to solve her problem. Your friend is the only one with the solution. With the Rose in place between the two of you, you will become a better listener and may ask better questions that can assist your friend in climbing out of her own hole.

Also, don't get stuck on "seeing" the Rose. Many, many successful, intuitive people using Energy Tools never "see" in their mind's eye. We all have our own unique way of brushing our teeth and we all have our own unique way of using these tools. Many people never "see" a thing; they simply *know*. Others *remember* what a Rose or other tool looks like; others *sense* it and still others *smell* it. One woman we know never "saw" a single image but smelled everything she worked with. She was fondly teased as being able to "read with her nose."

You may find it helpful to practice using the Rose tool prior to when you actually need it. Take some time when you are Grounded, in the Center of Your Head and Flowing Your Energy to just remember a Rose. Practice placing it in front of you, changing its color and moving it around.

The most effective time for using this Energy Tool is prior to entering a conversation with someone. Remembering the tool during the conversation works better than if not used at all, however prepaving or preparing in advance is always a better idea.

●●●

Another time this tool came in handy was about a year after my experience with Leena. I was still in the same office, managing the same flow of paper, people and priorities. One day I was rushing to meet a deadline. Four o'clock was quickly approaching and I was leaning over my drawing table, completely consumed in the project, focused only upon the demands of the moment. My assistant was at his computer, working as well. Suddenly my boss entered our office "Roxane, I'd like you to meet Moe." I turned my back to the drawing table to politely greet the new "marketing pro," Moe. Now, let me describe Moe. This is just so you may imagine the scene clearly. Rest assured, I have no opinion about him. Moe was about three inches shorter than I am (I'm 5'8"), quite stocky with dark curly hair and he spoke with an East Coast accent. Moe's white, starched, tailored shirt was unbuttoned almost to his belt. He had thick hair on his chest and flashed a heavy gold neck chain and several rings. Get the picture?

When I turned to meet Moe, I was cornered against the drawing table and was unable to step around and put a comfortable distance between us. Moe stood about one foot in front of me. He grinned broadly and eyed me up and down. Twice. You know the look. That simple action hit my solar plexus (power and control) and abdomen (sexuality) so hard I felt physically ill. In fact, his energy was so strong and intrusive I would have tipped over backwards if I hadn't been wedged against the drawing table. I politely smiled back and put the Rose between us to disrupt his pattern of zapping women (or at least from zapping me). Instantly, Moe took a step backwards and began speaking with the only other man in the office, "How 'bout doz Raiders?" Moe never knew what hit him. It was just an innocent, little, pretend Rose.

Chapter Nine

Blowing Bubbles

We must be the change we wish to see in the world.

Mahatma Gandhi

So there you are, stuck at the top of the escalator in Chapter Seven, paralyzed and unable to take your first step onto the moving stairs. Fear grips your body and your mind seizes up. You're 40 years old and on a business trip with a co-worker. What has happened? A strong, well-established belief (escalators are deadly) has bubbled up to the surface of your awareness and you are experiencing its effect. The old fear has returned to haunt you. Here's another example of this phenomenon. An adult who is afraid of dogs doesn't think of the fear until he sees a German Shepherd. Then the charged memory of his childhood dog bite is stimulated and causes him to respond in a way that doesn't benefit him now.

Frozen and sweating at the top of the escalator, in a busy airport, with hundreds of others scurrying about, you have a choice. You can either hunt for the back stairs, ask your co-worker to carry you down the escalator, or use an Energy Tool to release this belief pattern of fear. First, the theory behind it (to satisfy your Analyzer).

Our limiting beliefs can be likened to many jars resting upon a shelf. Each jar contains an uncomfortable or painful experience that fostered a belief about who you are and what you can have or be in this life. For example, one jar contains the experience and charge of when you were nine years old and the other children wouldn't invite you play kickball with them. Another jar holds the memory of when your first love cheated on you and lied about it. We have many, many of these painful experiences tucked away in jars.

One method of releasing these painful memories and the corresponding belief you've been carrying around, is to open the jar, smell it, roll around in it and deeply, strongly, re-experience every aspect of that uncomfortable event. You may get angry and cry to allow your Emotional Self to re-experience the pain. You may analyze all the minute aspects of the event in order for your Mental Self to re-live it. You may even get sick to your stomach or get a headache so your Physical Self can feel it all over again. Then, at some point in the process, which could take moments or years of work, you will let out a long sigh of relief and your Spiritual Body will release the pain and all four aspects of you will find peace.

Personally, I didn't enjoy the painful experience the first time it happened and I don't care to re-feel it all now. There is another way to experience the same result without as much discomfort and drama. You could choose to simply see the jar sitting on the shelf and say, "Oh, I see. That's the time my mother said she wished she'd never given birth to me." Then you could take it off the shelf and dispose of it, unopened. You can actually go to the sigh of release without re-experiencing the pain mentally, emotionally or physically. If you allow your Spiritual Self to do the work, you can bypass the pain. But...here's the clincher: No one can do this for you. You can indeed continue to pay $100/hour for months or years for someone to listen while you complain and re-live an uncomfortable childhood, or you can simply blow the bubble of belief, take the jar off the shelf and get on with your present-time life. The choice is yours. Only you can heal yourself.

Energy Tool #7
Releasing Limiting Beliefs

This tool is best used prior to an event that may trigger an old limiting belief. For example, *before* you find yourself frozen at the top of the escalator with a dozen impatient people behind you. However, if you do find yourself in a situation where the memories and feelings are flowing over you, this tool will work equally as well.

Since you are now familiar with using the neutral, easy-to-pretend Rose, we will use this image again. As you know, any image toward which you have positive or neutral feelings will work.

1.   Get yourself into a quiet, noise-free space. This may mean Flowing the Rivers of Energy through your channels for a few minutes at home in the morning or simply finding the Center of Your Head and Grounding behind your closed office door.

2.   Become comfortable in the Center of Your Head and own this space. Have a seat in your imaginary director's chair. Imagine looking out the front windows. Your eyes are closed for easier focus.

3.   Before you, about twelve inches away, just imagine or remember a Rose. Imagine its stem and petals. Make the blossom white or clear.

4.   Think of a limiting belief that you know affects your life (see page 76 for possibilities). This is the perfect tool to use to release those nasty NITs you've been discovering.

5.   Hold that belief in a bubble or ball in your imaginary hand in the Center of Your Head.

6.   Call into this bubble all the charge around the belief pattern. Just pretend the bubble is filling up and enlarging.

7.   When the bubble of belief is solid and full and charged, place it into the Rose out in front of you.

8.   Watch what happens to the Rose. Notice what color it turns. This is the energetic vibration, represented as a color, of this belief in your body and energy field.

9.   Give the command to the Rose to collect up this color and belief that may be lodged in your space.

10. Simply sit in the Center of Your Head and watch this Rose do its pre-programmed job. It may move around and through you or simply work from a stationary position in front of you.

11. When the Rose is finished, you'll know it. Visualize moving it off to one side. Explode it or imagine it zooming off into the atmosphere. The point is to imagine it completely disappearing. What is happening when you do this? The energy that has been collected up is going back to where it originally came from, in a more neutral state. And you have lost one more layer of charge on the issue.

This Energy Tool works. It works because whenever you place a faster, brighter energy or thought form next to a slower, duller thought form, the latter is consumed and eliminated by the former. Imagine lighting a candle in a dark room. The candle is now very noticeable and bright. It is vibrating faster and higher, so to speak, than the darkness. Now, if you move this bright little candle next to the sun, you no longer notice the candle. Now all you notice is the brilliance of the sun. The brightness of the candle is consumed by the greater brightness of the sun. In other words, when you take a slower vibrating energy and place it next to a faster, higher vibrating one, the former is consumed, loses its power and is no longer noticeable or influential. This same dynamic occurs with any type of energy, including the energy of belief patterns. Any lower, slower belief pattern, whether it be fear of escalators or "I'm really dumb," will be consumed by the brighter, higher energy of the Rose.

•••

Some time ago I was visiting a friend and spent the night in his spare room. This bed had head and footboards. My bed at home was simply a futon on the floor with no boards or railings surrounding it. As I was drifting off to sleep, my foot lightly brushed the footboard and instantly a flood of memories returned to me, unsolicited. These were events I hadn't remembered since the they originally occurred some 30 years ago. I re-lived the times when I was twelve, lying in bed with my feet touching the footboard. I began to notice uncomfortable feelings such as embarrassment and sadness bubble up. I remembered the experience of being the tallest girl in the school, skinny, flat-chested and clumsy. As the memory was flowing over me, I realized I could either really get involved in the painful emotions or release the charge. Fortunately I saw this moment as a perfect opportunity to release body-image beliefs that were now bubbling to the surface. As I lay in my friend's bed, I allowed the memories and feelings to move through and out of my space, along with the charged pain and beliefs connected to them. I also used the preceding tool…over

> The Rose vibrates at an extremely high frequency. Bruce Tainio of Tainio Technology in Washington State developed a bio-frequency monitor and measured the human body and foods to determine the relationship between frequency and disease. He discovered that a healthy human body electrically vibrates at between 62 and 68 MHz. Rose oil has a frequency of 320 MHz. (7)

and over. In less than six minutes I was able to return to a neutral state of being and release many long-held charges and judgments about my body. Another layer of false beliefs was peeled away.

●●●

You may notice that even after you use this tool and release a limiting belief, when you find yourself in that situation again, you may still have the charged response. What's up with that? The intensity or charge of the belief didn't just happen over night. It took years for you to fashion the life you have, so please be patient. It may take a few times and a few roses before you notice a change in response. Be easy on yourself and remember you are peeling layers of false beliefs from your onion to reveal the sweet kernel within.

Sometimes people look for a magic pill that will instantly relieve their pain. No magic pill from someone else can ever completely, permanently relieve your pain, nor change your pattern. Only you can do that. No one else can blow bubbles for you.

Possible limiting beliefs you may discover:

Stupid	Fat	Unattractive
Should be perfect	Lousy artist	Need to control
Guilt	Fear of success	Resistance
Judgment	Competition	Fear of failure
Victim	Clumsy	Please others
Will lose money	Unlovable	Abandonment
Not worthy	Should work hard	Not enough
Fear of rejection	Always wrong	Slow

Chapter Ten
Cloaking Device

Any fact facing us is not as important as our attitude toward it, for that determines our success or failure.

Norman Vincent Peale

Your boss or significant other is in a rotten mood and the rest of the office or household feels the effect. The word gets out and everyone steps to the side to avoid them. Or perhaps you're in a crowd and become uncomfortable with the closeness. There might not be any strong emotion or energy being directed at you specifically, but you feel a bit too close for comfort. What's happening? Your boundary or energy field is being influenced or pushed against. It might be a very slight, accidental intrusion, but you notice it. An adjunct to Energy Tool #6, the Rose, is what we call the Octahedron.

●●●

One weekend, Mitch drove down to San Francisco to visit a friend. They had several things planned, including a walk in Golden Gate Park, lunch and shopping in China Town. Now, Mitch lives in a small town about 150 miles north of "The City" and crowds are not something he finds himself in very often. The walk in Golden Gate Park was great, lunch was delicious, but shopping in China Town became a challenge in space management. Mitch found himself getting impatient and desiring to stop the excursion. He quickly became over-stimulated and wanted OUT. His politeness and desire to spend this time with his friend, however, assisted him in realizing that he was the one feeling uncomfortable, not the crowds around him, nor his friend. Since he knew he was the master of his moods and feelings, Mitch decided to feel good, rather than lousy and irritable. He remembered his Octahedron. Seconds after he erected this pretend structure, Mitch calmed down and stopped resisting the jostling about. His mood shifted and he began having fun again. Soon people actually stopped bumping into him. It was as though a feel-good force field had been created and he was able to enjoy the remaining time with his friend.

Energy Tool #8
The Octahedron

The Octahedron disrupts the flow of noise from 360 degrees around you. It establishes a type of impenetrable force field that keeps you feeling good and unaffected by the crowds, the noise or the rippling waves of energy.

1.   You may employ this tool with your eyes open or closed. It will work either way. A key here is neutrality. The more neutral you can become, the greater the effect.

2.   Visualize a marker at the edge of your personal energy field (18-24 inches), out in front of you at 12 o'clock. This marker may

be a dot, flower, flag or whatever neutral symbol you wish to use. I suggest you designate one symbol or image and use it consistently for the purpose of this tool. Doing so adds power to the tool. Because the energy field of success surrounds roses, I use that image.

3.   Place another, identical marker behind you at 6 o'clock, on the edge of your energy field. Hold your attention on, or be aware of both points simultaneously for a few moments.

4.   Place an identical marker to your right, at 3 o'clock and another out to your left at 9 o'clock. Hold your awareness on both points.

5.   Very intentionally, notice all four points.

6.   Place another identical marker above your head at the edge of your field and another about 24 inches below your feet. Hold your attention on these two points for a few moments.

7.   Very intentionally, slowly and deliberately check in with or say "Hello" to each of these six points. See if you can be aware of all six simultaneously.

8.   Now connect the points with lines. Draw four lines down from the point above you to the four points surrounding you and draw four lines up from the point below you to those four points surrounding you. You have created the Octahedron, one of five sacred geometric shapes called Platonic Solids.

This is practice in Mindfulness.

●●●

I enjoy visiting hot springs. A few autumns ago I went to Sierra Hot Springs in Sierraville, CA. I needed quiet time alone to reflect and retreat. One dusk, as I was meditating in one of the pools, a very enthusiastic and boisterous group of friends entered. They were enjoying the waters in a way quite different than I was enjoying them. The happy bunch began playing with each other, laughing, splashing and talking, moving about quickly and creating great waves that rocked my relaxed body to and fro. My quiet, neutral mood continued however, and I decided to take this opportunity for a little experiment. Not moving from my position, or even opening my eyes, I erected my Octahedron. I soon found a distance of approximately three feet around me to be undisturbed by the waves and rippling water. I smiled inside and out, settled back into my space and appreciated the friendly chatter from an attitude of gratitude and appreciation.

A few moments later, I decided to play again. I further experimented by extending the field out further and discovered that the further I extended my Octahedron, the quieter the pool became. When I finally opened my eyes some ten minutes after I began the experiment, I found myself to be entirely alone in the pool again. The group of friends had left and moved on to another location.

Chapter Eleven

Ascension
Made Easy-er

Misery is optional.   Jim Self

You are moving toward and preparing for ascension. This isn't as mysterious as it sounds. Ascension doesn't have to mean leaving this planet, taking your body with you and hanging out with Isis or Saint Germain. Ascension is an everyday occurrence. Ascension is when we leave one mode of being and rise into another higher, faster, purer one. It is when we make changes in our perspective, our preferences and our way of moving through life. We can say, at these times, we are moving from the third dimension toward the fifth. In a very real way we are. The fifth dimension is a place where what you think very quickly manifests. You might already be noticing that what you barely ask for you receive…faster and faster. As we make these evolutionary changes from a slower, denser vibration to a faster, lighter one, everything we have become familiar with also evolves. If the human race hadn't taken its steps into a new awareness, we'd all still be thumping our chests, grunting and looking like Neanderthals.

As we ascend toward the fifth dimension, we step up awareness in all aspects of who we are. Emotionally, we become less volatile and more joyous. Mentally, we experience balance between our brain's hemispheres and an integration of our intuition and analytical skills. Spiritually, we awaken our creative genius. As we take these steps toward total integration and alignment, we may experience a number of symptoms. You may be aware of all or some of these. Since you are reading this book, you are probably aware of several.

Ascension Symptoms

1.   Friends you've known for a long time are appearing different to you. The things they are interested in and are excited about, or the things they talk about, are not as interesting as they used to be. In fact, sometimes you find yourself looking at them and wondering, "Do I know this person? They seem so different." The fact is – they are not different. You are. You are beginning to shift your focus from the things and concerns that were very dominant in your life to areas and interests quite apart from the old ways.

2.   You are spending more time alone, and enjoying it. This is a time of quiet introspection or just a time of doing nothing. You prefer an evening reading or simply sitting on the back porch, over just about anything else. Watering your flowers has found new satisfaction. You prefer the small and simple pleasures.

3.   Because you are observing your friends and life quite differently now, you may also experience the feelings of sadness or loneliness. It is as if you know you are graduating from high school and going off to attend a college far away. The emotions you experience now are a bit confusing because they don't seem based on reality. Your friends are still there, you are still employed, the town looks (to your physical eyes) just as it always did, yet there is something

different, something "other worldly," and you know you are no longer relating to it as you once did. Do you remember a time you gave notice at your job and knew you would be there an additional two weeks? You felt a separateness and sadness, yet excited and anticipatory. You knew you would soon move on.

4. Work isn't exciting anymore. Work and career may be successful, but the passion is gone. You know another opportunity is drawing close. It is just within arm's reach, but unseen. It may feel as though it will rock your world and, although this excites you, there is a slight edge of apprehension. And you know there is nothing you can DO about it anyway, until IT reveals itself.

5. Food doesn't appeal to you as it used to. Perhaps you find yourself simply not eating until late in the day or eating less quantity. You may or may not lose weight as this happens. The type of food that you are now attracted to is quite different than it used to be.

6. Your body feels unusual. Perhaps it is as though your body has changed sizes, although your clothes still fit. Perhaps you feel taller.

7. Your sexual appetite has changed. Usually subsided. This may or may not concern you, but when you really evaluate it, you enjoy this shift.

8. Your vision may be slightly different. Colors may be brighter. The greens of grass and leaves begin to appear brighter, more yellow and vibrant. You may also experience an eyeglass prescription change.

9. Your sleep pattern changes. You may become unusually restless at night or have unusual dreams or want to sleep during the day. You may find yourself staying up late at night, or getting up very early. Or both. You may need less sleep.

●●●

Dee was experiencing many of these symptoms. She was "weepy" and didn't know why. She felt lonely, yet still had friends. Work no longer held her interest, although it wasn't dissatisfying.

Her body seemed to be going through something and just didn't respond like it used to. Nothing was working, yet nothing had changed. When she brought her attention to these symptoms and saw them as relating to each other, she understood they were communications from the wiser, broader part of herself. Dee gave herself permission to simply experience them and not make them fit into a logical structure. She grew to simply allow this energy to move through and around her life. She pivoted her perspective from "Something's wrong with me" to "This is just energy that's bubbling up and out. Soon I'll be back to feeling ease and passion." This took the pressure off and she began to actually enjoy tracking her progress. Dee stopped seeing these "weird feelings" as a problem but rather as positive signs of her expansion into wholeness. She stopped resisting her natural evolution. Ease and amusement returned. Dee is now setting a long dreamed-of plan into motion. She is returning to the coast to write.

●●●

If you are experiencing any of these symptoms, please know that this can be a result of using these Energy Tools. You are allowing energy to run through your system and move out the old patterns. The tools were designed to change your life and that is exactly what they are doing. You haven't entered the Twilight Zone. You are simply moving to a place that includes more of you and less of the noise that isn't you. Congratulations. We call this time between worlds a "**Growth Period**." It is a time to celebrate. Your body and mind and emotions may, however, not agree. Even though a Growth Period is a time to congratulate yourself on your spiritual progress, sometimes when we enter this phase of growth, it hits our physical system as something uncomfortable.

Once we make the personal commitment to change our life situation, it is as though the mighty *construction-crew-in-the-sky* hears our thoughts and jumps to respond. "Okay guys, lunch break is over. Jill, down there, wants to clear out all the pain she's been carrying around that has kept her from finding a partner. Let's hopto, grab your tool belt and help her drag it all up from the bottom so she can toss it." Or, "Alright crew, Jack is asking for our help. He wants to return to physical health. Hey guys, everybody pile on down there and show him all the crap in his life that doesn't match his desire so he can clear it out. He believes he only has a short time left, so speed it up boys and give it all to him at once."

Sometimes we resist the changes. You may discover your body, mind and emotions doing unusual things. You may bump into walls, want to sleep more, feel irrational emotions, lose your keys and wallet, put the stapler in the refrigerator, put your underwear on backwards. It's okay. This is just a Growth Period. Laugh at yourself and be easy. Give yourself a break. This is a time to nurture your body and give it what it wants. You see, what is happening is you (as non-physical or Spirit) are taking huge leaps in your evolution toward freedom. Your slower, denser, physical system (body, emotions, mind) is working hard to keep up. Make it easy on your total self and treat the denser parts well. Go for walks, sleep in, pet the cat, lie around and do nothing, have more sex, watch movies, have less sex, eat something special, take a bath. Take care of yourself. If you resist this important time, it will only become more uncomfortable.

You may see your physical self as a cherished pet cat. You feed and pet your cat, make sure she's comfortable and happy; you hold her and scratch her in all the parts she likes to be scratched. And she gives back to you. She purrs and kneads your legs and rubs her forehead on yours. If you treat your body as you would a special pet, it will then allow you to make these steps into the next dimension much smoother.

Take a nap. It's only energy.
It will be over soon.

Let yourself drool.
You are not alone.

Chapter Twelve
Zapping the Toaster

*It's not whether you get knocked down;
it's whether you get back up.*

Vince Lombardi

Years ago I shared a very small office with my assistant, Dave. Dave would very often begin his day in a foul mood and by 11 a.m. he was cussing and demonstrating his frustration. Dave also claimed to have "irritable bowel syndrome." (Probably just a coincidence.) During his mornings of imbalance and emotion, his computer also seemed to malfunction, which would only add to Dave's frustration. The relationship between man and machine would escalate and intensify until the machine eventually won out and would completely crash.

Perhaps you've experienced a tape recorder that doesn't tape the lecture or consultation, even though it was tested prior to the event. Then there are the light bulbs, recently replaced, that blow out or the printer that keeps jamming during a hectic deadline. Electrical appliances are sensitive to electrical impulses, sometimes extremely sensitive. When one electrical device is charged and running at a higher than usual frequency, other electrical devices in the vicinity increase their frequency in an attempt to entrain to it or match it. In other words, like a tuning fork, an electrical device that is vibrating stronger can influence others in close proximity to also vibrate at the same or similar rate.

This vibratory match also occurs with those electrical devices called people. Have you ever attended a meeting and noticed who dominated the energy and how they did it? If there is one participant who is extremely out of tune with the others and is strongly throwing his opinions and ideas out among the group, some members of the meeting are bound to match him. What begins as a productive meeting quickly escalates into a gripe session or a thick, uncomfortable silence. The participants move from personal balance to imbalance as they match the tuning fork. It's all energy in motion. Becoming irritated by this strong personality also counts as "matching" because you leave your state of balance. You are affected by his energy and move into a personal state of imbalance.

●●●

I was enjoying a dinner at a restaurant in Spokane recently and observed a table of women dining nearby. The six ladies were quite obviously enjoying each other, the conversation and the food. They were well matched with each other and having a great time. They flirted with the waiter, shared food and laughed freely. One woman in particular seemed to have the best stories and jokes and the others were frequently deferring to her. She set the tone of the get-together. As the dinner continued I observed the mood of the party shift. Although I didn't hear their conversation, the voices became softer and less enthusiastic. The leader was sharing a subject of concern and frustration. She was affecting, like a tuning fork, the other women and they were matching her. The women were now picking at their food, staring off into the distance and frowning more. I would catch occasional words and they changed from eagerness to dissatisfaction, seriousness and grief. Two of the women were even in an emotional debate. The strongest tuning fork was setting the tone for the party and the party shifted energy to match hers. They all stopped having fun.

•••

We are well trained to match or empathize with others. When we are in a charged situation, we either match it (and argue or complain along with them) or we leave the room. Most electrical devices can't get up and leave the room, so they tend to match the stronger charged electrical device (you) and malfunction in some way. It's all energy and everything seeks balance. Just like the toaster that only burns the toast when you're in a hurry and very hungry.

That's also what Dave's computer did. It matched his high emotional charge and was simply showing him where he was out of kilter in his own electromagnetic field. Dave never understood that fact however, and continued to blame the computer for his frustration. In fact, I later found out he would be complaining about the computer even before he got to work, preparing for disappointment and aggravation, which always arrived quite obediently.

Observing Energy

When an electrical device begins to malfunction in your environment, stop, look and listen. What out of balance and dominant energy source could possibly be causing this effect? Is there a human involved? What condition is the human in? Is he balanced and aligned in his energy field or not? If it's you that is operating this device, evaluate your alignment and balance. That device is just matching the operator, or the strongest electrical pulse in the environment.

What to do if you discover you are indeed the one out of balance:

1. Simply take a break, a nap or a walk. Remove yourself physically from the equipment until you regain your balance and alignment.

2. If it is inconvenient to distract yourself with some activity that is more enjoyable, you can regain your balance by simply going to the company restroom, and taking a seat. This also works right there at your desk. Just briefly close your eyes and push your chair away or turn it so you create a bit of distance between you and the misbehaving piece of equipment.

3. Check in with your Grounding Line. Make sure it is still attached. You could cut off the old one and put down a new one. Give it the command to magnetically attract to it any out of balance energy or attitude that is in your experience now.

4. Notice the emotion or feelings pulsing through your mind and body. With your imaginary hand, grab a bit of what is racing by and throw it down your Grounding Line.

5. Use the Making Separations Tool in Chapter Fifteen.

6. Intentionally think about or remember something that feels better. Choose something that has absolutely nothing to do with the current predicament. When you pivot your thought, your mood, energy and resulting experiences also pivot.

7. Staying in the Center of Your Head, visualize a Grounding Line attached to the piece of equipment. Command it to release any energy that is off kilter.

I guarantee, if you take these precious few moments, the computer and the rest of your day will unfold with ease.

Chapter Thirteen

THE FOUR FACES OF YOU

These bodies are perishable; but the dwellers in these bodies are eternal, indestructible and impenetrable.

The Bhagavad Gita

Phillip, Emma, Mendelson and Spatia have been room-mates for many years and are continually learning how to live together in peace and cooperation. Each is a very strong-willed individual and has well-defined agendas, passions, abilities and desires. It is the beginning of Spring and all four roommates want to throw a party. This is a perfect chance for each of them to demonstrate creativity and genius. The challenge they face is how to pull off a successful party for their guests, while still allowing each other full creative expression. You see, Mendelson's idea of good music is classical, softly played in the background, so the guests may talk and discuss interesting topics. Emma wants to play music that stirs the emotions and draws people to move and dance. Phillip, who tends to dominate, believes it's important to show their guests the abundance and good taste they have, while Spatia likes to keep it simple. As you can see, each roommate has his or her own opinion about the best party to throw. Can these four diverse personalities join forces and pull together a party that satisfies them all as well as their guests?

•••

You, too, have four very unique, individual aspects that together compose who you are as a total being. You have an Emotional Self, Mental Self, Spiritual Self and Physical Self. Full Self-Integration requires all four aspects to be recognized, satisfied and respected. They all must be honored and given what they need to become and remain healthy. This integration brings balance into your outer and inner life. The emotional, spiritual, mental and physical selves are like legs under a stool. If out of balance with each other, the stool topples over and anything resting on its seat is overturned. A party designed by a group of conflicting, disjointed roommates can result in discomfort for all involved.

A person who allows her Emotional Self to dominate her life is ungrounded and may consistently create drama and chaos in her life. Something is always "wrong" with her. Her personal challenge is neutrality and focus. A person who is allowing his Mental Self to dominate his life may experience a lack of warmth that prevents friendships from forming or he may worry excessively and focus predominately on the future. His challenge is judgment. A person who allows his Physical Self to dominate may be underdeveloped mentally and emotionally and finds his body to be his only concern. He may love the material and become obsessive or despondent when his body ages or fails to operate the way he expects. His personal challenge is greed. A person whose primary focus is upon the non-physical or spiritual aspects often has a difficult time understanding the ways of the world and relating to others. The needs of the body, mind and emotions may be neglected and ignored. Isolation is this person's challenge.

Another way to imagine these aspects is to recognize they represent the four quadrants of your brain. Dr. Paul MacLean, former head of the Department of Brain Evolution at the National Institute of Mental Health, refers to the r-complex, or reptilian cortex, as the portion located at the brain stem. It is concerned with survival, territory and procreation. This is also called the "Lizard Brain" by Glynda-Lee Hoffmann in *The Secret Dowry of Eve* (8). It is where your Physical Self lives.

The limbic system or mammalian cortex is located on top of and surrounding the r-complex and is the home of the Emotional Self. The rational mind, or neocortex, is the familiar, convoluted mass of gray matter. It is where the Mental Self lives and is the intellect, analyzer and reasoning center. The prefrontal cortex is located directly behind the forehead and is also called the frontal lobes. It is the home of your intuitive or Spiritual Self. It is the portion of the brain that science has barely discovered, yet has been a part of our human anatomy for up to 200,000 years.

All four aspects are essential for a complete human experience. To deny or emphasize one over another creates an imbalance in the entire system and the four-legged stool topples to the floor. An effective way to balance and align these four aspects is to personify them. As an adult kindergartner, just pretend these four parts of your brain and your personality are roommates with unique and equally valuable contributions to offer. Together they can create the best party ever conceived.

The Care and Feeding of Your Four Selves
The Emotional Self

Personified, this aspect of you can be a young, immature child whose emotions are quite evident. Imagine a child who is allowed to fully express her energy-in-motion, e-motion. She is non-verbal and so must express her needs through dreams, behavior patterns, acting-out and will power. She cries, perhaps not understanding why. She laughs at the silly things. This child is volatile and unpredictable. She feels vulnerable at times and impassioned at others. Sometimes the Emotional Self (let's call her Emma) feels misunderstood, not cared for and disrespected. How she communicates this is often erratic and not generally understood by the other selves. When Emma tries harder to be heard, the Physical and Mental Selves push harder to quiet her. Emma internalizes her fire and sooner or later, this smoldering fire of energy-in-motion manifests in ways the other selves feel even more uncomfortable with.

If your Emotional Self is not allowed freedom, she will eventually affect the Physical Self (Phillip – this is kindergarten, remember) by causing physical pain or illness. The Mental Self (Mendelson) may experience confusion and mental unclarity. When this small whimpering child turns into a big, out-of-control beast, Mendelson and Phillip can no longer ignore their discomfort and must allow Emma to contribute to the house party (your life experience) in ways she enjoys.

A healthy and respected Emotional Self enjoys her job. Here are a few items in her job description:

1. All emotions – those stimulated from both internal stimuli and data and those in response to external data and events.

2. How we feel about ourselves in general, if we like, value or respect ourselves.

3. The feelings of conviction we attach to our beliefs.

4. The parent/child bonding relationship.

5. Intimate emotions with a significant other.

In addition to simply recognizing your Emotional Self and personifying her, what else can you do to assist this part of you to come into alignment?

1. Establish a line of communication with her. Talk to her and discover what your Emotional Self enjoys and needs.

2. Stimulate emotions and observe them as they move through your experience. Watch movies that evoke emotions, and not just the socially acceptable ones like sadness or love. Rent a movie that stimulates fear, irritation or anger and notice where in your body that emotion lives. After the movie, you may want to make separations from it by Grounding the movie from the uncomfortable body part, using your Grounding Line.

3. As you notice comfortable or uncomfortable emotions rise to the surface, verbally tell someone (your dog counts) what and where the emotions are. You may not have words for them. That's okay. Just get as close and specific as you can. This validates your Emotional Self and helps her feel accepted.

Learning to heal your Emotional Self can be illustrated through Ben's story. Ben was experiencing the frustration of a six-year divorce process. Looking at Ben, one saw a very grounded, quiet, gentle man. He admitted however, that he could get spontaneously angry and that side always frightened him. He felt out of control and was afraid he would hurt someone. While using his Energy Tools of Flowing Energy and Grounding, Ben personified Emma (his Emotional Self) as a ferocious dragon, guarding her hoard of treasure. He gave Emma permission to exist and express herself. Ben talked to Emma and allowed her to fully be who she is. When his Emotional Self finally heard a "Hello" and was acknowledged, she had permission to express herself. In a very short time, through an easy, safe, nonthreatening and playful imagery process, Ben and Emma became friends. The resistance Ben previously experienced as fear and doubt vanished.

Ben's Emotional Self communicates with him now through slight, non-painful sensations, particularly in his belly. This is Ben's clue that his emotions are activated and have some information for him. Ben's increased awareness and appreciation for this aspect of himself has opened a door of communication that allows him to recognize when he is on-track or off his path. Ben is able to recognize strong emotion before it gets out of control. His relationship with his Emotional Self is now active, safe, healthy and creative. Ben is noticing that he laughs more and can get angry without the accompanying urge to hit something. During our work together, Emma transformed from a fierce dragon to a lion, to a German Shepherd, to a Golden Retriever, as Ben continued to allow that energy-in-motion to simply be okay.

Ben also released a good deal of resistance toward his ex-wife, Suzie. As Ben recognized and allowed his resentment and anger toward her to exist, with no resistance or judgment, it became unnecessary for him to express it. Ben simply noticed the emotions rise and fall in his body as sensations and stiffness. Within a very short period of time, the ex-wife came to an easy agreement with Ben. Because Ben released the resistance and the charge he was holding, the pattern of relating to Suzie was disrupted and she no longer had anything to push against. She completed the divorce paperwork quickly and was soon on to her next relationship.

The Physical Self

Your body was designed to move and work. Bodies love to be active. Unlike the Emotional Self, we are allowed to express ourselves physically. You can personify your Physical Self in a way that currently represents your relationship with your body. Is it a big strong muscle-man, perhaps encumbered by his massive bulk? Is he small and bird-like or large, flabby and weak? Allow Phillip (your Physical Self) to appear and act as he truly is. Phillip's job is to survive and he does it with a passion. He only thinks about and directs his focus upon those things that either help or hinder the survival of the system. Like the Emotional Self, Phillip is non-verbal and so must resort to expressing his needs through behavior patterns, acting out, sensations and movement.

Here are some items in his job description:

1. Establishing, patrolling and marking territory (buying or renting it, putting up the fence, security lights).
2. Fighting to defend territory (football games, job competition).
3. Foraging and hunting (shopping, research, crime detection).
4. Homing (heading home after the hunt or with news).
5. Hoarding (collecting art, coins, food, money, cars).
6. Use of defecation posts (telling dirty jokes, especially those having to do with bodily functions).
7. Formation of social groups (teas, luncheons, staff meetings, church committees).
8. Grooming.
9. Courtship, mating, breeding and tending to offspring.

Your Physical Self must be allowed to do his job with gusto and creative permission, or he is restricted and unhappy. If he is limited in some way from keeping the system safe and healthy, he may either push against the other selves, or weakly submit to them. In the former case, he may appear bulky and bullish, aggravated and loud. If he has surrendered to the pressures of the Emotional and Mental Selves, Phillip may grow thin or flabby and weak, quiet and pale. Either way, Phillip is out of balance and not expressing his wisdom from a place of alignment. If your Physical Self is ignored or abused for long enough, the Mental and Emotional Selves will surely begin to be affected. Perhaps you know of others who have been out of communication with their bodies for so long they no longer look or act their young age, are emotionally bitter or mentally fatigued.

Because the physical body is undeniably real to our five physical senses we sometimes give it more permission to run the show. It occasionally receives more of our mental and emotional attention than is necessary. When the body talks to us, it is easy to jump to the conclusion that "something is wrong", rather than to ask, "What are you trying to tell me about my level of balance and state of being?" Have you ever been at work when others are talking about "cold season" and all their aches and pains? When you happen to sneeze, they say, "Oh dear, you must be getting sick too." That is a very important moment for you. You have a big choice. Do you believe the group agreement about colds and your body's state of health? Or do you laugh, walk away and choose to be well? If we do jump to the belief that something is wrong and focus our attention there, something may indeed become wrong, even if it was previously healthy and whole.

●●●

Jim was lecturing in Colorado a few months back and a student noticed a patch of rough red skin on Jim's arm. The student was a dermatologist. "I know what that is. It's melanoma cancer." ZAP! Programming in the making. Jim had a moment of pause and chose not to buy the program. He thanked the student, asked his body what it needed and put some essential oil on the spot. It disappeared within a week. The student was surprised, to say the least.

●●●

Several years ago Sam began his dream of writing a novel. A very short time into the project, he began to experience severe joint pain. It eventually hurt most of the day. After about three days of this, Sam found his Mental Self focusing on "What if this is arthritis or carpel tunnel syndrome?" The battle to manage worry became constant. Sam found his Emotional Self becoming sad, hopeless and disappointed. He also noticed NITs pertaining to his ability to write and publish his book. With very little assistance, Sam sat down to communicate with his body and find out what it was really trying to tell him.

Sam's father used to write short stories and actually had a few published in magazines. He wasn't as successful as he would like to have been, however. Dad didn't get much support or encouragement from the family. This was quite disappointing and frustrating to him. His creative genius was never satisfied or fully expressed. He was stuck creatively. Our arms and hands contain our creative channels. The pain Sam was experiencing in his hand was connected to his dad's stuck creativity and his mom's belief it was a waste of time. She had suffered from painful rheumatoid arthritis for years. Sam chose to change this pattern of belief. He simply pretended the Life Force Energy from his front channels was fully flowing down his left arm and gushing out of his fingers and palm. Sam imagined many different colors just for fun. In about 15 minutes the pain stopped and never returned. Sam's body was simply telling him there was a limiting belief around writing and creativity stuck in his arm channel. It was just energy. Sam could have easily embraced the belief that he had crippling arthritis and was destined to suffer forever. It's only energy.

●●●

In addition to recognizing your Physical Self and personifying him, what else can you do to help him return to balance?

1. Allow your Physical Self to move and express himself. Dance, walk, and stretch. Notice, as you consider this activity, if you experience resistance. It's not necessary to hurry and join a gym and sweat until you can't move. Simply take your Physical Self on a date. All your body may want is a walk around the block.

2. Notice all the physical things around you. Use all five senses: sight, sound, taste, touch and smell. Experience each as fully as you can. Really push your nose into that flower until it's covered with scent. Get really close to the bark of a tree and see all the tiny crevices. Listen for the crickets over the television. Suck a lemon!

3. Love your body. Tell each body part you love and appreciate it, as you rub on lotion in the morning. You might notice here, too, if any NITs pop up.

4. Feed your physical body what it likes. Sometimes determining what that may be is tricky, as we live in a vortex of programming

around food and bodies. Many times, our relationship with food is intertwined with the Emotional and Mental Selves. A method to re-establish a line of clear communication is to play with muscle-testing techniques or the pendulum. (See References and Resources.) These tools may temporarily bridge the communication gap between your physical body and the rest of you. As you continue to say, "Hello" to your body and pause to listen, your natural lines of communication will clear.

5. When you are sitting quietly or Running Energy, visualize your body standing in front of you. Notice the places it is imbalanced or uncomfortable. This is not an intellectual process. Just imagine what the body in front of you might be indicating. You may be surprised at the locations that light up. Thank the body and ask it what it needs to feel appreciated.

6. Open your Grounding Line and leg channels about 10% more and run extra Earth Energy through them. Sometimes the resistance or pain you experience is from pumping 220 volts through wire capable of only 110 volts (metaphorically speaking). Simply open the channels a bit to allow more juice to flow, resistance-free.

The Mental Self

The Mental Self can be likened to a large and powerful sledgehammer. This sledgehammer is a perfect tool for pounding nails and knocking out two-by-fours. Because it is so capable, and because we live in a very intellectually validating culture, we ask this sledgehammer to do jobs it's not suited for. Your Mental Self (Mendelson) is very eager and willing to do what it is asked. He will sometimes create a rationale for why his is the right method. For example, if you ask the sledgehammer to frost a cake, it will think it's doing a great job and try to convince you of it. The cake, however, isn't going to look or taste appetizing. Cool and rational, logical and sensible, Mendelson is certain he can do any task at hand and if the result is less than optimal, it must be because of an external problem. It was served too late in the party, no one likes chocolate, and the pan wasn't the right shape.

This attitude is bred into him through generations of belief patterns. This can really impact the other two Selves and cause great confusion, discomfort and disharmony. If your Mental Self muscles his way into projects or is invited to participate at a level that is over his head (pun intended), he may take control and lead the proceedings. Your Emotional Self is denied her unbridled joy and enthusiasm and your Physical Self may suffer pain from neglect. Many times your Mental Self will ignore the other Selves until the entire system is threatened by a breakdown or broken body through "accident" or illness. Perhaps you know someone who allows their Mental Self to dominate their life until they are in tremendous pain. Something must change or the entire system suffers. Many people, when they contract a life-threatening disease, receive great insights and change the patterns of their lives. Some of them survive the experience.

●●●

Bea was married to George for just a short time before they began having babies. They were devout Catholics and had six children very close together. George was unhappy in his low paying job and drank heavily. Many nights he would return home after midnight and take his frustrations out on Bea by pushing her against walls and beating her up. Over twelve years, she received many broken bones and bruises. Bea always rationalized his behavior and made excuses for his foul mood. "George is just having a temporary set-back. He's depressed. He really is a good person." Bea had many logical reasons to stay married. "It would break my mother's heart if I left George. The church does not sanction divorce. The kids need a father."

George continued to beat her, eventually in the presence of the children. Early one morning he returned, drunk as usual, and not only slapped Bea, but he began threatening the eldest daughter. It was then that Bea's Mental Self could find no other logical reason to stay. She had reached the darkest level of emotional and physical pain in her life. She was willing to tolerate her own pain, but it wasn't until her daughter became the recipient of George's abuse that Bea was able to pull her Selves together and change the situation. It finally became obvious that her Mental Self didn't have a clue about how to handle this situation.

•••

Your Mental Self's job description includes:

1. Takes external information and processes it to make logical, rational sense according to information already stored in its experience-banks.

2. Language. The Mental Self can verbally communicate its needs, interpretations and perceptions.

3. Processes the symbols that evolve into writing, reading and mathematics.

4. The analyzer. Loves to figure things out, prove theories and fix problems.

In addition to recognizing your Mental Self and personifying him, you can encourage him to develop his strengths by offering him the following:

1. Recognize and write down jobs that he is good at. Validate him, verbally, for his fine work in his areas of expertise.

2. Give him specific jobs to do such as balancing the checkbook, reading maps and making to-do lists. Make this a conscious act and intentionally engage your Mental Self.

3. Recognize when he has stepped into the realm of controlling the emotions and body. Simply being aware of current patterns of mental involvement will assist in balancing Mendelson's enthusiasm and return him to only those areas in which he is proficient.

4. When embarking on an activity that involves only the Emotional Body (an intimate moment with a lover, meditating) or Physical

Body (digging the garden, washing the car), ask your Mental Self to wait outside until there is work for him to do. You could also visualize an analyzer shut-off switch in the Center of Your Head. You might find yourself turning it off many times at the beginning. That's okay. Beginning to use this tool is similar to working out at the gym. You are developing a muscle you haven't used much until now. Don't expect it to lift 150 pounds at the first attempt.

5. Notice people around you who are dominated by their Mental Selves and how they're experiencing their lives because of it. Are they emotionally at ease? Are they happy and healthy?

The Spiritual Self

Spatia is a unique addition to the creation of this house party and your life. In fact, without her, the party wouldn't unfold smoothly and harmoniously. Spatia doesn't lift the tables with Phil, plan the activities with Mendelson or even choose the music with Emma. Spatia oversees the entire operation and is the spiritual supporter of everyone. She makes sure they are all doing what they love and are receiving the validation and encouragement they deserve. Your Spiritual Self recognizes and intuits all needs and questions. She helps direct each Self to the best solutions. She is the quiet, invisible force in the background that holds the whole party together.

Your Spiritual Self has been there, in the background of your experience your entire life. Spatia is quiet and not usually recognized by your five senses. Science and many individuals have denied her existence since patriarchal societies began to dominate the planet many centuries ago. She never dominates your life, but insists on working with the other aspects for an integrated self. Self-Integration includes increased awareness, intuition, insight and communication between the four bodies or selves. Only your Spiritual Self can facilitate this. She is clearly connected to your ultimate source of information and Light. As the planet and all her inhabitants evolve toward full four-body integration and alignment, Spatia is recognized and appreciated. Schools and individuals come forth to assist in developing Spiritual Abilities and offer tools for greater awareness and intuition.

Spatia's job description goes something like this:

1. Provides a super-sensory overview of the entire mind-body-emotion connection.

2. Harmoniously coordinates all three denser aspects, recognizing and capitalizing upon the strengths of each.

3. Responds to personal and social information, as opposed to the sensory stimuli which the neocortex (mental), limbic (emotional) and r-complex (physical) respond to.

4. Focuses attention upon the inner worlds of creativity and potentials (personal growth).

5. Increases awareness of our inner and outer selves. Self-awareness.

6. Intuition and insight.

7. Cooperates with the limbic system, gut feelings and the ability to identify with the experiences of others. Compassion.

8. Foresight and planning for the future. This ability allows us to make more far-reaching and globally effective social decisions, aware of possible consequences.

9. Altruism.

10. Unleashes the creative human spirit.

11. Recognizes and stays in communication with your Higher Self, Soul or Supreme Being.

12. Assists in anchoring Light into the four-body system.

To play with your Spiritual Self and develop your Spiritual Abilities:

1. Practice Energy Tools in a focused, intentional way to quiet the noise in your life and develop your intuitive abilities.

2. Return to a quiet space and imagine your Spiritual Self standing before you. Ask her to help you communicate clearly with your emotional, physical and mental bodies to give them what they need. The answers may arrive sometime later and in a most unusual way.

3. Go to a public place and watch people. Act as if you are intuitive and notice what information you get from watching.

4. Become aware of your physical, mental and emotional messages. Many of them are messages from one aspect of you to your Spiritual Self. As you continue to get quiet, clear out the noise and listen, the messages will become clearer and louder.

5. If you already notice many voices in your head, know that only one of them is your Spiritual Self. As you use these tools, the others will eventually clear out and the quietest one will be yours.

6. Begin a Spiritual Record. Include insights, desires and night dreams, meaningful quotes from your readings, drawings and any-thing else documenting your unfolding Path. This process focuses your attention on your goals, validates your Spiritual Self and is helpful to review at times when you might feel discouraged or "stuck."

7. Make written notes in your Spiritual Record of all the synchronistic events in your day. As you recognize and validate them, the quantity and quality will grow.

8. Bring beauty into your life. Beauty is the language of Spirit. Create beautiful spots in your office, home, yard, and car. Play with Feng Shui.

9. Ask and intend to visit gardens, parks and libraries or attend a lecture on a specific subject while you sleep.

10. Record your night-dreams immediately upon waking, even if they make no sense. Doing so will increase their frequency and clarity.

11. Most importantly…Have fun and laugh a lot. Your Spiritual Self finds your life amusing and entertaining. So can you.

Chapter Fourteen

Cutting tHe Cord

*The paradox of control is simple. The more we try to control life,
the less control we have.*

> *Joan Borysenko, Ph.D.,*
> *Minding the Body, Mending the M*

Recently I worked, via telephone, with a teenager, Linda, from the East Coast. Her mother had received a session a few weeks before and hoped I could "fix" her daughter. Jan was raising her daughter alone and wanted to be sure I knew all the details of what was going on with her daughter.

When Linda called, she sounded like any typical 15-year-old girl with braces. She was intelligent and intuitive, responsible and capable. She knew what she loved in life, and desired great achievements. I asked her to explain briefly what was going on and what she would like work on. She questioned why she was not getting along with her mom like she used to. We began to work on making the transition from childhood into young adulthood a bit smoother.

Unlike in the animal kingdom, when a human child is born, it cannot survive alone for many years. The child and mother therefore energetically agree to create an invisible line of communication or "Survival Cord" between them. This cord benefits them both. The child has a way to survive more safely and the mother gets the experience of full motherhood and intuitive communication with her child. This cord can be created between the father and the child as well, if the dad is the primary caregiver or if the father is emotionally closer to the child. For our purpose, we'll simply assume it is Mom to whom the child is corded. If you've ever had a child, you may remember times when you were sound asleep and your infant was in bed in another room. The child would roll over in his sleep and the next thing you knew, you would be standing next to his bed, wide awake, checking on him, automatically, without even thinking about it, as if he reeled you in. He did. Because of this Survival Cord, your body sensed the movement and brought you to his bedside. Many lactating women have the experience of their breasts dripping between feedings. This is the child communicating to her, through the cord, "I'm hungry." This energy cord is a wonderful device, perfectly designed for both the parent and the child. The baby is able to get his needs met and the tribe survives.

This Survival Cord doesn't stay attached indefinitely. Or, rather, in healthy parent-child relationships, this cord doesn't stay attached forever. I have seen many adults with this line of communication still firmly connected. Perhaps you know of a man who is still a momma's boy, or a grown woman who is still very much involved with her parents' lives, with no life of her own. The cord is still attached in these cases. An analogy would be the telephone receiver that hasn't been replaced on the cradle after the conversation has ended. The loud buzz is an irritation to the system of both the parent and the grown child.

There is a natural and perfect time in the child's life, when she no longer needs the safety and security of the Survival Cord. In fact she will want to disconnect it to survive on her own, or at least experiment with surviving on her own. In tribes and cultures where children and their rites of passage were honored and celebrated, this was an important and powerful time for the entire community. Today, however, this time of disconnecting the cord can be a time of stress and misunderstanding for everyone involved, including the greater culture. This period of time is called adolescence. It is a time when the child takes her greatest steps toward adulthood.

Linda was experiencing this natural step toward adulthood. She was also experiencing stress and worry about her relationship with her mom. Linda was very familiar with this cord. Every time she worried about Mom, argued with her or took steps toward independence, her solar plexus hurt. This was where the cord was attached now and every time Linda tried to remove it, it ached. The emotional, physical and mental resistance to this cord removal and impending independence, was not only Linda's, however. Much of it was her mother's. Jan's fears about life and her desire to protect Linda from the pain she had experienced as a young woman caused her to keep a good deal of attention and worry on Linda. Jan wanted to keep this invisible cord attached. In fact, Jan needed this cord for her own emotional survival more than her daughter did. As Linda would jiggle and test this line and make efforts to remove it, Jan would notice the shift. Her fears, worries and dependency would flare up and she would make stronger attempts at keeping the cord attached, and Linda controlled. It was literally a tug-of-war that was physically and emotionally uncomfortable, manifesting as stress, self doubt and stomach aches for both of them.

With very little instruction, Linda began to gently, slowly, respectfully and lovingly loosen the cord. Two minutes into the work, our phone line went dead. While I waited for Linda to call back, Jan came to mind along with her anxiety, worry and loving concern for her daughter's well-being. When Linda called, I asked her what happened. "I don't know, the phone just went dead and Mom was standing at the door, asking me if I got disconnected." Interesting choice of words, I thought. Indeed, that's exactly what happened. As the cord was loosening, Jan noticed, energetically, the change in Linda's connection with her. Just like times when Linda, the infant, rolled over in her crib, Jan was aware of the shift. This time, however, she became insecure and uncomfortable and created a situation that stopped the removal of the cord. Jan had been vacuuming and "accidentally" pulled the telephone cord out of the wall socket. There are no accidents. Linda understood this was just energy between herself and her mother. Instead of continuing the process, I gave Linda instruction on how to gently disconnect the energy cord and gradually transition into young adulthood with greater ease. Both she and Jan could now make the change with less physical, emotional and mental conflict.

Releasing the Survival Cord doesn't mean you won't have a mother or child anymore, or that the two of you won't love each other. What it does mean is that each of you will now have the freedom to move and create and design your life the way that pleases you, while you support the other person and her journey. You both can now bump your nose, scrape your knee and experience the empowering act of picking yourself up. This is one of the greatest gifts parents can give a child; the freedom to stub her toe, learn from the experience and create a better way that works uniquely for her.

An interesting side note: Six weeks later, Jan called for another appointment. Some changes were occurring that Jan didn't understand. Linda was no longer angry and rebellious. She was doing better in school and Jan was feeling alone and abandoned. The previous relationship pattern was breaking up and Jan was confused. She learned to reduce the size of her end of the cord and was soon able to find her inner stability without depending on her teenage daughter for security.

Energy Tool #9
Releasing a Cord

Releasing the Survival Cord can be done from either end. Either the parent or the child can begin to disengage this line of attachment when it is no longer needed. It isn't advisable to do so prior to adolescence.

1. After Grounding out your daily noise and finding the Center of Your Head, become aware of where this cord is attached. You do this by noticing what part of your anatomy may have uncomfortable sensations when this person (as in teenager) is pulling away from you, or is acting overly concerned and worried (as in parent). The Survival Cord may be attached to any chakra area (base of spine, lower belly, solar plexus, heart, throat or head). It is different for every body and every relationship. If you are not sure which body part or chakra is connected, just go with your first inclination. You can't make a mistake here. If it is a parent/child relationship you're working on, pretend the cord runs between first (base of spine) or third (solar plexus) chakras. If it is a love relationship that you're working on, just pretend the cord runs between fourth (chest), second (lower belly) or first chakra.

2. Once located, simply imagine a cord attached from this spot and extending out into the air in front of you. You are not concerned about disengaging it from the other person, just about making your own separations and reestablishing your own balance. Visualize what the attributes of this cord might be, its shape and diameter, color and texture. You might notice, with amusement, if your analyzer gets involved here. If so, just ask him or her to sit this one out.

3. Very gently and slowly, pretend you are making the diameter smaller and narrower. You may use your physical hand if you like.

4. Over a period of a few sessions of decreasing its diameter, it will be a very simple matter of gently jiggling it loose or unscrewing it. The longer you take in this process, the smoother it will be for

everyone involved.

Death and Divorce

Have you ever had the experience of losing a loved one either from death, divorce or abandonment and felt the pain in your body? The physical location of this discomfort is where you shared a cord with this person. Terry lost the love of his life to cancer several years back and he suffered for many months from severe pain in his solar plexus. He described it as feeling as though something was ripped out of his gut. Something was ripped out – her cord. In order for a person to take their Next Step, whether that is passing back into the non-physical or divorce, they must collect up their attention and energy from where they left it. That means disconnecting their cords and moving on.

You may look at it this way: if you have ever moved out of a marriage, you either took the physical things you were attached to, or decided you didn't need them anyway. If an object *did* hold great meaning to you and you left it behind, a portion of your attention and energy would remain there with it. That portion of you is not with you now and is not available for your personal use. To make complete separations from someone or something, one must either be in possession of 100% of their energy and attention or be neutral and uncharged about what they did leave behind.

You may use the Releasing a Cord tool to make the important changes that will enable both of you to take your Next Steps. Another Energy Tool to experiment with is Making Separations.

Chapter Fifteen
MAKING SEPARATIONS

In releasing, you let go of the clinging, and you are made whole again. In releasing and honoring what has been, there may be tears, but there will also be doors opening to future possibilities.

quote from Jesus,
Love Without End, by Glenda Green

Paul attended one of my free classes in Idaho and stayed after the others left to ask a personal question. Paul had been planning a vacation at a golf resort in Washington State for some time when a new acquaintance invited himself to attend and share a room for the weekend. Paul is a very polite and considerate man, always conscious of the feelings of others, sometimes to such a degree that he allows himself to be taken advantage of. His weekend was only two days away and Paul was finally embracing the truth of the situation. He wanted no part of this other man. Paul said Glen was unkind, selfish and loud. Glen was not aware of boundaries and consistently stepped into Paul's comfort zone. Glen was also quite needy, controlling and clingy around Paul, and Paul wanted to use this weekend for introspection and quiet personal time. He was in a quandary. How does one get his needs met without hurting others or retracting commitments? We sat down together for about 15 minutes to talk and work. I introduced the following tool and moved Paul through it step by step. We parted ways and I never expected to hear from Paul again.

The next morning, as I was scanning my e-mails, I noticed one from Paul. When he returned home from the lecture the night before, he retrieved a phone message from Glen. Something more important had come up in Glen's life and he couldn't attend the golf weekend after all! Interesting how energy works.

●●●

In Chapter Two, the Grounding Line was introduced, which is an excellent method to release noise from your life. It also works with noisy people. Here is another method to remove a particular someone from your mind and field of attention. It also works when you have moved on to the next item of business and found yourself still thinking about the previous one. Now you can make separations from others whom you find yourself thinking about long after you have left their presence. Many massage therapists and psycho-therapists find this a helpful tool to complete the session with one client before they begin to work on another. Doing so keeps the therapist from accumulating and holding all her clients in her awareness. By the end of the day she won't feel like an opossum with all her babies on her back, or a kangaroo carrying her offspring in her pouch. Keeping a person in your conscious awareness or even in your subconscious awareness does not benefit either of you.

Energy Tool #10
Making Separations I

1. Take a few private moments to clear away some of the noise from your internal environment.

2. Be in the Center of Your Head. Anchor here and get comfortable in your imaginary director's chair.

3. In the area 12 inches in front of your face, imagine or remember a white Rose.

4. Think of someone who is irritating you or just consistently on your mind.

5. Visualize putting him in this Rose and watch what color the Rose turns. That is the color of his energy in your space. This is not "bad" energy. It just doesn't belong to you. He wants it back in order to feel whole again. So do you.

6. Give the command to this Rose to collect up all of his energy and this color from your space.

7. One way you can do this is, imagine the Rose below your feet. Ask it to slowly rotate around your body, collecting up all of this energy that isn't yours.

8. When the Rose reaches a point above your head, thank the person, think of one thing you appreciate about them (a tiny appreciation is okay here) and move the Rose away.

9. Explode the Rose or make it disappear. All their attention and energy will automatically return to them. Another option is to simply tell the Rose in front of you to collect their energy and color without moving from that location. When it is finished, you will know. Then you may thank the person, think of one thing you appreciate about them and explode the Rose or make it disappear.

10. Take a moment and completely replenish yourself with your Golden Ball of Light. Be sure to fill those areas in the physical

body that may have tingled or twitched or otherwise released this person.

It is important for the success of this tool that you remain as neutral and uncharged as possible. Sometimes when you are releasing other people or beliefs from your space, uncomfortable memories or feelings may surface. Sometimes the physical body experiences sensations. This is a normal indication that the tools are working. It's just energy and the more you can stay in the Center of Your Head, Ground and Run your Energy, the quicker those uncomfortable logs will be dislodged and swept away in the river.

Have you ever done or said something and then realized you sounded just like your mother or father? The "Making Separations" tool not only helps you release folks that might irritate you; it helps you empower those you love. Allowing a loved one his full independence and power is an invaluable gift. As you make separations from people in your life, you are returning their energy and attention back to where it belongs – with them. When someone has left his attention outside of his Six Points, it is as though he has scattered his one-dollar bills all over town. When it's time to buy food and pay the rent, there is nothing left. As your loved one leaves his energy and attention on you, he is operating on less than 100% and that doesn't feel good to him. So – the most loving thing you can do for your friend, child, lover, pet or the sales person on the phone is give him back his energy. In the process, you are also clearing your own body, mind, emotions and attention of what doesn't belong to you. You'll both feel more whole and empowered if you make separations.

•••

Jen enjoyed her daily lunchtime walks with Jeffrey, or at least she mostly enjoyed them. They talked about work projects, sports, pets and family dramas. Those were the parts Jen enjoyed. The aspects she didn't enjoy included Jeffrey's flirting and inviting her to have dinner with him. She liked him but not in a romantic way. In class, Jennifer used Jeffrey as the subject for this Energy Tool. The following day at about 2 p.m., I received a phone message from Jen. During their daily walk, Jeffrey "out of the blue" apologized for bugging her and hoped they could still be friends! Jen never spoke to him about her irritations, but simply gave him back the attention and energy he had left in her space.

•••

The other people in your life are not the only ones who scatter their energy and attention. So do you. Just like them, you don't intend to leave your attention and energy with someone else. You just may not be aware of what you're doing, you may want to help them or you may need something from them. And when you have left any amount of your attention somewhere other than within your Six Points, that power isn't with you. You've left your dollar bills all over town and now it's time to take your sweetie on a date. No dough - nothing left in your wallet when you need it. Here is another tool to give them the energy they left with you and to call yours back home to you.

Energy Tool #11
Making Separations II

1. Clear your space to play. Ground and Run Energy.

2. Be comfortable in the Center of Your Head.

3. Imagine or remember a white Rose.

4. Think of someone you'd like to return energy to.

5. Visualize putting him in this Rose and watch what color the Rose turns. That is the color of his energy in your space.

6. Create another Rose next to the first one. This Rose represents you. Notice the difference.

7. Give the command to your friend's Rose to collect up all of his energy from your Rose.

8. Give the command to your Rose to collect up all of your energy from his.

9. When the Roses are finished exchanging energy, thank your friend and explode his Rose or make it disappear. His energy will return to him where it can benefit him.

10. Now find your Rose again. Fill it with gold and allow it to enter your body. It has the wisdom to travel and refill your system with the energy it has just gathered.

11. Take a moment and completely replenish with your Golden Ball of Light. Be sure to fill those areas of your body that you may have noticed responding to the energy work.

Chapter Sixteen

Boonlert's Tools

By Lynn Jacobs

High school teacher extraodinaire.

*We've included this chapter as a testimony
of how these tools can change the lives of our
children and ultimately, the world.*

He entered my classroom one day at lunch, looking frustrated and a little scared. "Ms. Jacobs, I need help."

"What kind of help, Boonlert?" I asked him, quietly. "Do you want help with the Administration, or another kind of help?"

"Both, either one, anything. I don't know how much longer I can hold on. Some White Power kids are saying things to me and I'm afraid I'm going to lose it. Last night I had a dream that I went to C.Y.A. (California Youth Authority, a prison for juveniles) and when I got out I didn't know how to start my life. Can you just help me?"

Boonlert was a Junior in high school, and a member of a Southeast Asian youth gang. He had been deeply involved with his "crew" as he called it, but now he wanted out. He was a student in my Advanced English as a Second Language class, and earlier that year began to read on his own for the first time in his life. His interest in reading had been kindled by books we read together in class, and then blossomed into a personal love for books that was changing his outlook on life. His mind was opened to possibilities that never before occurred to him. He wanted freedom but didn't know how to get there.

The day he came to me for help, I could see that he was under a great deal of tension, and his desire to choose an alternative to gang warfare was real. I could also see that if he didn't find another choice of action soon, he could find himself in bigger trouble than he had so far experienced. His continued involvement in fights – not of his choosing anymore, but undeniable, didn't help in his change toward freedom. When he spoke of his frightening dream, I heard his Inner Being speaking to him. Together, we began a months long journey to save Boonlert from his own reputation and past actions.

On this day I made the decision to offer him some Spiritual Tools to help him defuse the barely controlled anger that too often got the best of him. I told him that I knew he could do hard things, and asked that he listen to what I was about to tell him with an open mind. He was to sit in a chair, and close his eyes. I told him to imagine a cord that connected him to the center of the Earth. Through this he could release all the bottled up energy that he held inside. I walked him through widening the cord into a tube, and flushing the toxic energy down through it. I then showed him how to make a Gold Sun over his head, call back his own clear energy, and refill his aura with it.

The last tool I showed him was how to use Roses. I had him stand up, and I walked toward him. When I got too close for his comfort, he was to tell me to stop. He did, while I was still quite a distance from him. Then I had him imagine a Rose halfway in between us, with a long stem that connected to the Earth. He was to see the Rose catching my energy and draining it away before it reached him, the stem of the Rose acting as a Grounding Cord for my energy. He told me when he was ready, and again I approached him, a step at a time. After each step I stopped, and waited while he relocated the imaginary Rose, keeping it halfway between us. We continued this until he felt I was too close. This time I could get very close without his feeling any discomfort. I explained that the purpose of this exercise is not to allow others to get real close to him, but rather to prevent their energy from bombarding him and throwing him off center. Others' energy could simply be drained off by that imaginary Rose before it reached him. I asked him to just try these three tools for awhile, and to report back to me in a week or so.

For the rest of that school year Boonlert battled with his public image and the changes he was making personally. He felt like a different person, and spoke often of the changes he was experiencing, both as a result of reading and of using the three tools I taught him. It took the outside world many months before they would acknowledge these changes, however. Boonlert came to my classroom nearly everyday for lunch, occasionally bringing someone he wanted to influence in a more positive direction. By the end of the year he pointed out to me that he no longer had any friends at school. All of them were either locked up, or running from the law. Later one of them would be dead, the victim of a drive-by shooting.

Toward the end of Boonlert's Junior year, I mentioned that it seemed that he might like to go to college. He looked at me in a funny way and said he'd just been thinking about that, for the first time. He didn't think it was a real possibility for him, however. Once again I reminded him that he can do hard things, the challenge being to stick with it until he succeeds.

We spent his Senior year getting him into the California State University an hour from his home, and finding him scholarship money to help pay his way. His grades were surprisingly good (he was number 44 in his class of 200). Boonlert won several scholarships, the most noteworthy being the "Peacemaker Award" offered by a local church congregation to the student who had made the largest strides in creating peace in his home, school and community.

Boonlert constantly felt brought down by his reputation as a violent troublemaker. He was therefore very surprised when, a couple of days after the scholarship awards ceremony, a stranger approached him in Wal-Mart, asking "Aren't you the guy who won all those scholarships the other night at the high school? Congratulations." He shook his head in wonder as he told me about this, saying "I never thought anyone would know me for something *good* I did."

A few weeks after graduation, Boonlert and I were out for dinner, talking about all the changes he experienced. I told him I was going to write this chapter for Roxane's book, and asked him to tell me about the tools and how he uses them. He explained it this way: "I sometimes feel like I'm so pressured, full of old dirty stuff. I close my eyes and imagine turning on a faucet, and it's like dirty water just flows out of me. I ground myself then, and fill up with fresh energy and I feel better."

When his friend was killed last fall, Boonlert didn't know what to do with the anger and sorrow he felt. He was afraid of losing his carefully maintained balance. He also worried about his personal safety, particularly when he was in his hometown on weekends. I reminded him of his tools, and the value of their use, (also suggesting that if he felt unsafe, to listen to that feeling and stay at college, not coming home on the weekend). I reminded him of his Grounding Cord to release the anger, and the Roses to shield unwanted energy from other people. He smiled and said that he hadn't forgotten, and he uses them all the time. Boonlert seems to be finding his way with grace through life's difficult terrain. I am proud of him and inspired by him.

College is not easy for Boonlert. After he finished his first semester, he called and told me he passed all but his English class. He was still proud of himself however, even of his progress in English. "When I started the semester I was getting ones and twos on my essays. Now I'm getting threes and fours, and I need a five to pass. So I'm almost there." What a change from the angry, frustrated young man I met two years ago. His head is held high, and he knows that he is in charge of his future. With his Spiritual Toolbox in hand, Boonlert is ready to tackle whatever comes his way. He is no longer afraid of doing "hard things."

Author Postscript :

A few months ago I was invited to speak at an East-West Bookstore *in Mountain View, California. When the lecture was complete and guests were mingling, I noticed a handsome young man shyly, politely edge his way up to me. I instantly recognized Boonlert and was honored to finally meet him. We both stood silent in a happy, full, timelessness. With grateful tears running down both our cheeks, we hugged "hello" and good-bye. Boonlert disappeared into the group of guests.*

Chapter Seventeen

Faceted Gems

Vision is the art of seeing the invisible.　　　*Jonathan Swift*

The rough stone was buried deep in the dirt. As we crawled through the obscured hole, we found her, covered and filthy, almost invisible. Until we brushed her off, she could have passed for a clump of tar. Once clean, it was clear we had found a stone most precious, although we didn't know her true worth. Climbing out of the hole, and sitting in the sun, the two of us pondered our array of treasures. This rock was different. Special somehow. It talked to both of us and stood out among the rest. We agreed to get an expert's opinion upon our return to the city. Gathering our belongings, we left the canyon.

A few days later Jamie again found the rough stone, this time under a pile of unwashed clothes. It still intrigued him and sparked his imagination. He brought it to the best jeweler in town. The jeweler looked it over very briefly. Almost too briefly. Jamie felt embarrassed that he'd brought a clump of tar to this professional and had interrupted his busy day. The expert evaluated it as a chunk of common quartz. Nothing worth more than a few cents. He tossed it back onto the counter. Disrespectfully.

Jamie then brought his stone to another expert; a woman who simply tumbled stones and cut them. She held Jamie's rough companion and said she'd like to see "What's inside this one." Reluctantly, the boy left it there, overnight, to pick it up in the morning. At 9 a.m., as the lapidary opened her shop, Jamie was outside. He was obviously anxious to see what had transpired. The woman was only interested in brewing her morning coffee.

What she finally placed in his sweating hand was not a clump of tar. It was not common quartz. The humble lapidarist gave Jamie a multi-faceted, clear and brilliant precious stone. She gave him Light.

●●●

Look at any cut stone. It has many facets, each surface reflecting a different image and light. So do you. You are a multi-faceted being. You are a lover and a gardener, an employee and employer. And behind every role is a system of thoughts and beliefs. You, the gardener, think quite differently than you, the office manager. You, the lover, hold thoughts quite different from you, the employer. Each facet is a part of your unique whole. Each facet reflects a unique part of who you are. Each facet is simultaneously enough alone and an integral part of the whole.

Remember when you were in kindergarten and you would place a certain hat upon your head to instantly become that role? You could be a firefighter, a pirate, a nurse or a cowhand anytime you wished. Same concept here, as an adult kindergartner. Let's say you have several personal issues fighting for your attention right now. Your partner is stressed and might be diagnosed with a disease; your boss is in a rotten mood, you feel fat and slow. Your mother is coming to visit this weekend and the house is a mess; you're worried about something you said to a co-worker and moments ago you were called upon to present a proposal at work. Impromptu.

Conducting a successful business meeting requires a certain, unique thought system and focus of attention. It is important to be in business mode at business and play mode while playing. You wouldn't wear your baseball cap to work, nor your work hat at home, however we do this all the time. We continuously wear inappropriate hats. We wear our relationship hat at work and are preoccupied with the drama at home, creating errors and low production. We wear our work hat to bed and wonder why our partner is not satisfied anymore.

Have you ever had the experience of driving to a destination and suddenly realizing you passed your exit? Your attention wasn't on the present-time task of driving. You and your attention were quite involved with something else. Many times we are worrying and fretting while we drive. The next Energy Tool will help focus your full attention on the current circumstance whatever that may be. This is a tool that brings your attention back to the needs at hand and sets the stage for greater success, whether at baseball or board meetings. Your family will enjoy having more of your attention on them, and you'll enjoy business more when a greater amount of your attention and creativity is focused there.

Energy Tool #12
Hats

For the purpose of this exercise, let's assume you want to become more focused at work.

1. Take a few minutes and have a seat. Close your eyes for greater

focus and be in the Center of Your Head.

2.   Breathe. Say, "Hello" to your Grounding Line. Give it the command to magnetically attract to it all the noise in your mind right now. Take a full minute or two to just sit there and release tension and noise.

3.   If you notice specific thoughts and bits of distracting noise in your mind, grab them and throw them down your Line.

4.   Imagine what your relationship hat might look like on your head. Just make it up and go with the first thing that pops up. Take that hat off and place it on the front seat of your car, out in the company parking lot. You can pick it up later if you like.

5.   Breathe and return to the Center of Your Head.

6.   Notice another hat you might be wearing that is not work related. In other words, what else is on your mind?

7.   Imagine what that hat looks like and place it outside.

8.   Continue identifying and removing hats until you don't notice any others and your mind has quieted down a bit. Here are some hats you might find on your head: sibling, mom/dad, son/daughter, student, boss, coach, party organizer, house-cleaner, plumber, computer guru, teacher.

9.   Visualize what a work hat would look like. Make it amusing yet professional. Place it on your head, using your imaginary hands. Make sure it's snug.

10. Tell your body to match the hat. Pause and notice anything and everything. Allow your body to adjust and move to match the intention of business. It may want to sit up or breathe.

11. Tell your mind or Mental Self to match the hat. Pause.

12. Tell your Emotional Self to match the hat. Pause.

13. Take a deep breath, open your eyes and move with Certainty into your presentation.

Telling your physical, mental and emotional bodies to participate and match your Hat is like asking a group of children to step up to the challenge and fully act their roles in the school play. The team is ready, on deck and prepared to work together for a common goal.

What is going on in your head sets the tone for the rest of your experience. You are what you think. Even truer than that is: *You are what hat you are wearing.*

Chapter Eighteen

Monday Morning, 7 A.M.

Supply is Spirit and it is within you.　　　*Joel S. Goldsmith*

The alarm rudely bursts into your dreamy world. A world similar to this one, only better. No stress, no deadlines, just gardens and libraries and peace. Trouble is, once that bell brings you back here, you don't remember much of that other world and even worse, the ease you felt is quickly being replaced with the "reality" of your day. Do you begin the day in enthusiasm and eagerness? Are you directing your day or is your day directing you? Do you find yourself at work, not exactly sure how you got there, asking yourself why you're there and what you've signed up for? Many of us find ourselves confused and questioning everyday.

Most of us are not in the habit of asking ourselves a very simple question: "What would truly make me happy right now?" We're not in the habit of asking that question, nor listening to the answer. If we did ask and listen, and then follow through with the action, our lives would indeed dramatically change. That can be revolutionary and perhaps a bit frightening. Sometimes it's easier to just stay as we are. Young children however, are on a mission to experience happiness. They remember the importance of following their "bliss," as Joseph Campbell calls it. They do what excites them at each and every moment. They ask themselves, "What would feel really good right now?" Not, "What would feel good someday when I pay off the car, get a job and find the right partner?" Many of us miss the bliss of the "now moments" as we reach for and live for goals in our uncertain future. Young children are adept at achieving this bliss each morning as they awake. That's their job.

> *Children are happy because they don't yet have a file in their minds called, "All the Things That Could Go Wrong."*
>
> *They don't have a mind-set that puts "Things to Fear" before "Things to Love."*
>
> *Unless we can be like little children, we can't enter into the kingdom of heaven. Unless we can be like little children, we can't be happy.*
>
> *Children are happy because they don't have all the facts yet.*
>
> Marianne Williamson, Illuminata

The alarm rudely screams again and you begin your day. You have the choice right now, lying in bed, all cozy and comfortable, to have the day of your choosing. What would you like to experience if there were no possibility of failure? As a child, you didn't know failure, so you just plunged ahead with your day, not knowing it was supposed to be difficult and full of parts you didn't like. You believed life was supposed to be fun and easy and that your job was to just play all day. You would jump out of bed, eager and bright, believing anything was possible. When did you decide you had to grow up and be serious? What would you choose in the first ten minutes of your day?

●●●

Ann was prone to depression. She never succumbed to drugs, but she did spend a lot of time alone, miserable, feeling sorry for herself. One day she had this experience:

Lying in bed one autumn Monday morning, all Ann could see out of her window were cold clouds, filled with impending rain. It was going to be a miserable day and she was depressed. Again. Ann, again, decided to stay in bed until "whenever." She remembered, as a child lying in bed and dreaming dreams of her future life and what it might be. None of it came to pass and that made this morning even worse. Ann also remembered how easy it was back then to do anything she wanted. Life was so easy with no responsibility: no children, no stupid boyfriend, no job she hated, no body that ached. Her body felt heavy, lazy and stiff, fat and immobile. Yes, Ann was going to stay in bed all day. And all night if she felt like it.

Drifting back to a half-sleep, Ann found herself asking her Self, "If you could do anything you wanted today, regardless of time, location or money, what would you like to do? Anything. This is just a game, Ann. It's not real – just go for it. We won't tell anyone."

So Ann thought, "Anything? If I could do anything I wanted, I would go for a walk and visit the neighbor's ostriches." She was surprised at the thought that just popped into her head. She could do anything regardless of time, location or money and she automatically chose to do something this simple? Ann lay there and realized that her body felt different with that thought. Somehow more at ease.

"Okay, Ann, that was a good start, what else, after the walk? Now remember, you don't have to DO any of these things. This is just a fantasy you're making up here."

"Okay. After the visit with the ostriches, I'd play in the garden. Weed the garden. Then I'd rent a movie and bake some apples." Ann checked in with her body again as she watched these strange thoughts pass by. Her body felt lighter, even a bit happier. (She was careful to not think that last part too loud.) With that, Ann realized she wasn't depressed anymore and actually wanted to get out of bed and visit those strange birds. She did.

Ann still gets depressed and feels sorry for herself. She still gets into those miserable states and wants to stay in bed all day. And she does stay in bed all day – for about 10 minutes. Then she plays the fantasy game she made up and begins her day with eagerness.

Now, that Bedroom Fantasy game may work for Ann. She obviously doesn't have to go to a regular job on Monday morning. What about the rest of the world? What about you, who still work every Monday morning? Even though you may spend the day in an office, it *is* possible to make the day yours. You may not be able to visit the ostriches or bake apples, but you can experience the same freedom and eagerness. Try this:

Energy Tool #13
Bedroom Fantasy

1. When you wake up in the morning, don't get up. Give yourself about five minutes to set the tone for the day. These first few minutes of your morning can positively or negatively influence your entire day.

2. Just lie there.

3. Begin to become aware of the good feeling things that are already happening to you. The cat is loving you up, the cloudy sky makes the room feel cozy. The rain on the roof sounds melodic. The weight of the comforter is soothing. Notice what already feels good, right now.

4. When you get to that good-feeling place, very gently move your attention to something you know is going to occur during the day

in the office or at home. Purposefully imagine the events unfold with ease and amusement and success. Just pretend everyone involved is having a great time and the results are win-win for everyone. Be as detailed as you can, while still feeling those good feelings. Make it fun.

5. Occasionally you will notice your analyzer, "Yes-Butting." The NITs will go something like this: "It will cost too much and take too much time. You're too old or too fat. You don't have a Ph.D. You're married/single and just plain tired." Bring your thoughts back to something that feels better. Distract yourself with the purring cat on your face or the music of the rain.

6. Return to your Bedroom Fantasy when you're feeling good again. Expand upon it. Let it develop for a few moments of pure, undistracted imagining.

This tool takes only a few minutes in the morning. It is very "kindergarten" and simple. Yet it will literally change your life. When you first begin using this tool, the Yes-Butting and NITs may loudly begin after only a few seconds. It's okay. You're breaking up some extremely well ingrained belief and behavior patterns here and it may take a couple rounds. Most people can only hold the pure, undiluted fantasy for less than five seconds the first time. Just laugh at yourself and do it again tomorrow morning. Soon, you'll be able to hold a fantasy, undistracted for ten seconds. I know that you don't think ten seconds is very long. Just try it for yourself and notice all the noise and NITs that want to distract you. You'll discover ten seconds is a very long time, indeed.

•••

Jean took a beginning seminar several months ago. Her strongest desire (outside of a relationship) was to earn more as a psych-nurse. She enjoyed her job of serving others and she was good at it. Nursing was her calling; she just wanted to be paid what she thought she was worth. That's not an unreasonable desire, unless you're living and working in a town with a strong cultural agreement to remain small and economically challenged. Jean attempted every ploy she and her friends could think of, logical and illogical. Nothing seemed to convince her supervisors she was worth more. She finally surrendered and began focusing her attention on what she *did* love about her job. Jean appreciated certain other nurses and many of the elderly people that she served. She made medical suggestions to the doctors and felt validated by the increasing number of doctors who adopted her suggestions. Although Jean wanted to earn more money, she was also willing to take responsibility for her own part in this creation. She knew she still held limiting beliefs around prosperity and abundance. She continued to use her Energy Tools to release and transform these old beliefs into new patterns of thought that benefited her.

Jean's parents lived in Napa Valley for a number of years and still own property there. Occasionally Jean would accompany her mother on trips back to visit old friends. While her mother visited and socialized, Jean would wander around town, walk in the park, cruise the tourist stores and explore alone. This continued for several years and Jean grew to look forward to her mother's trips. Jean began to fantasize about what it would be like to live near these foothills and among these vineyards. Jean used the images and emotions she gathered in Napa as a tool to fantasize about what she wanted to create and experience in her future dream home, dream relationship and dream job. She was in no hurry and had no objective other than to feel good in her fantasies, right now.

About three weeks into the seminar, Jean missed a class and called the next day with this story. A friend of her mother's had passed away a few days before and Jean drove her mother down to Napa for the memorial. While the service was being conducted, Jean slipped away for an hour of fantasy data gathering. She happened to pass a hospital that she never noticed before and stopped in just to poke around and gather ideas for her "mock-up." She stopped at the front desk and the Human Resource Director *happened* to be filling in while the receptionist was out briefly. Jean introduced herself and chatted about the local area and nursing. He told her of a job opening that she would have fit into perfectly. It had, unfortunately, just been filled a week ago. He suggested she complete an application regardless. She did. The HR liked what he read and he said he would like to interview Jean if she had time, right then and there. She did, indeed. During the interview, he mentioned that he wasn't pleased with the way the new employee was working out and he would like to create a new position just for Jean. If, that is, she would like to work there. She did, indeed. And he hired her right then and there. At nine dollars an hour more than what she was currently earning!

On the drive back home, Jean told her mother about this "miracle." Her mom asked if she would like to move into the small cottage they own and haven't rented for several months...rent-free. Jean did, indeed. She left town last Sunday, with Energy Tools in hand, to truly experience the dream she's been building.

●●●

Another version of the Bedroom Fantasy can be employed during your daily, focused quiet time, while Grounding and Running Your Energy. You may return to this fantasy anytime, add to it, fine tune it and adjust it to fit your present time dreams.

Energy Tool #14
Focused Fantasy or Mock-Up

1.   Spend some time quieting your internal noise. Ground and Run Your Energy. When you reach the feeling of quietly cruising, then proceed.

2.   From the Center of Your Head, look out in front of you.

3.   Imagine or remember a large bubble or balloon.

4.   Inside this bubble imagine all the details of the event or object or experience you wish to create. Be as detailed as possible. If you

are unsure about some of the details, just guess. Although you want to be detailed, it isn't necessary to be technical and analytical. This is not an intellectual exercise.

5.   Add a Grounding Line to the bubble and give it the command to drain out opinions of others or thoughts and beliefs that may prevent it from occurring. It's not necessary for you to recognize these opinions or beliefs. Just trust that the Grounding Line will magnetically attract and release them.

6.   Continue to play and focus on your fantasy. Imagine what it would be like the moment you receive this thing. Allow yourself to experience the emotion of joy or satisfaction, anticipation and success. Fully enjoy the emotions you may receive during this fantasy.

7.   Notice where in your body this emotion lives and allow it to move and grow fuller - expanding into other areas of your body. Let yourself smile at the possibility of actually experiencing this fantasy. Feel it fully.

8.   When the Grounding Line is finished draining, you will intuitively know. Cut it off and let it drop it to the earth.

9.   Fill the bubble with gold.

10. Remember the feeling of gratitude.

11. Release the bubble and allow it to zoom off into space, or---

12. Imagine this bubble exploding high above the earth and all the many pieces drifting down to the places necessary to create it. (Don't try to figure out where they go – just allow the bubble to do its job while you watch from the Center of Your Head.)

As your fantasy unfolds and begins to appear in your life, you may get the feedback that the Mock Up isn't quite right. You would like a green car, not a white one. No problem, the next time you are doing your energy work, just recreate the fantasy and adjust it accordingly. The longer and more purely you can hold this fantasy in your mind's eye without distraction or mental Yes-Butting, the stronger the message will be sent to the construction-crew-in-the-sky. Once those guys really "get it," you will too. All they need from you is a clear, undiluted message with a big punch of emotion. Emotion is the fuel that drives your dream to the finish line.

•••

Dave and John were sales reps for a printing company I hired many years ago. Dave was married with two young children and he radiated satisfaction. He would visit me on his route and tell me the fantasy he and John would spin out together as they drove up and down the West Coast, selling printing services. Over the many months together these two guys had fantasized all the details of starting their own print brokerage firm. They had a great time designing the logo and name. They window-shopped on their trips to the Bay Area for the perfect location. They even decided what computer equipment they would buy and who they would hire in the office. They were just "messing around and day dreaming." Both were very satisfied working for their company.

One day Dave came in looking very dark and depressed. Three days before he had been laid off. "Downsizing" they called it. Dave was worried about finding work and supporting his growing family. He left my office in a miserable mood. A few days later I heard John quit.

Three weeks later Dave visited my office unexpectedly. He was glowing. He and John decided the lay-off was a blessing instead of a failure and took it as the opportunity to start their brokerage business, "for real." They did and it is still incredibly successful. And they thought it was just messing around. I guess the construction-crew-in-the-sky heard them.

Whatever things you ask, believe that you have received them and you will receive them.   *Mark 11:24*

Ask and you will be given, seek and you will find, knock and the door will be opened   *Matthew 7:7*

Chapter Nineteen

Color Your World

We must learn to reawaken and keep ourselves awake, not by mechanical aids, but by an infinite expectation of the dawn, which does not forsake us even in our soundest sleep.

Henry David Thoreau

Kate was twenty-three, slim, blonde and very attractive. Her dream was to get a Ph.D. and she was having a real tough time staying focused. Up until now, Kate had only been validated for her physical appearance and never for her intelligence. Her low self-esteem attracted friends who supported her negative beliefs. They partied a great deal and Kate began abusing drugs and alcohol regularly. This pattern eventually got her arrested and placed on probation for many months. It was during this time that she joined our Mastering Certainty class. Kate was committed to changing her life and freeing herself from old patterns. Life was too uncomfortable for her the way it was.

Part of Kate's probation included appearing before a judge and checking in with him about her program, which included service work and group therapy sessions. These appearances in court always made Kate nervous and confused. She would lose her confidence and self-worth before the judge. Up until now, she always dreaded them and made herself sick with worry prior to the date. During class she learned to set her crown chakra at a color and word and allow the rest of her system to match that tone. Two weeks after the last class I got a call from Kate. She met with the judge the day before. "How did you do, Kate? Did you remember your tools?"

"Yes," she said with enthusiasm. "I sat in the car first and set my crown at blue and Certainty. I thought of Audrey Hepburn and how Certain she always was. I entered the courtroom as usual. When it was my turn, I stepped up to the judge, like I always do, and do you know what he said to me? The judge said, 'Well Kate, you sure look Certain today!'

Kate now attends the university and is working part time. The last time I saw her was at the natural food store! She looked – well – she looked Certain.

●●●

The crown chakra is located at the top of the head, right where the soft spot is in a baby's skull. It is related to the Pineal gland and the brain. The Spiritual Ability of "Knowingness" lives here. This is the ability to know, recognize and own your personal Truth.

This is an extremely powerful ability and it affects all the others in a mighty way, much like its corresponding endocrine gland. When you manage your seventh chakra and intentionally set it at an energy that benefits you, your entire system, inside and out, physically, mentally and emotionally matches that intention and functions under that direction. You may choose to walk in Certainty and Presence or Depression and Stress. It's all up to you and where you set your crown.

Energy Tool #15
Colors and Words

1. Begin by getting into your Running Energy mode. Sit in the Center of Your Head, within your Octahedron.

2. Think of a personal attribute that you'd like to experience today. See the list on the next page for ideas. What color does that word represent? Choose the first color that pops up. You can always change it later if you wish to.

3. Notice your crown chakra. Touch it if necessary. Visualize this spot in the color of your word. You may imagine painting it with a brush if that works for you.

4. Now write the word on your crown.

5. Ask your body to physiologically match that color and word. Pause. Notice how it feels. Allow your body to adjust to fit this new energy. It may want to straighten up or smile.

6. Ask your Emotional Body to match that word and color. Pause and allow it to soak in. What emotion do you notice?

7. Ask your Mental Body to match that color and word. Notice if your level of focus or chatter shifts.

8. Recall a person you know who demonstrates this personal attribute. Observe him move and talk and interact with others. Notice his relationship with his body. Watch how he remains within his boundaries. Notice his level of self-integration. Observe how he demonstrates this word and vibration.

9. Imagine yourself moving around like him and allow your body, mind and emotions to move in the chair and adjust to match his aspect.

10. Without filling up with Gold or bending over, simply stand up into this energy and begin to move around slowly as if this is who you really are.

You can be, if you choose.

Aspects of you:

Amusement	Certainty
Presence	Grace
Personal Power	Class
Creativity	Balance
Abundance	Ease
Peace	Joy
Connection	Grounded
Sophisticated	Intelligent
Beautiful	Professional
Humorous	Happy

▲

Chapter Twenty

The Business Meeting

What we will play with in this chapter may have been way over your head a few dozen pages ago. That's great. I hope it still is. It's way over most of our heads. In fact, that is why it works so well. Our heads are not involved. So far, you've learned to move out the noise and focus your thoughts to a finer degree. You've learned to recognize and maintain your boundaries and not be affected by the drama around you. You've learned to remain stress-free while standing in chaos. Here is a hypothetical situation where you can now apply all you've learned so far.

There you are, a to-do list as long as your daughter's right leg and it's time for another meeting. Which is it this time? Interdepartmental? Production? Marketing? Who cares anyway?

They are always the same – uncomfortable and laborious. How can you make this one different – more enjoyable or at least more tolerable?

A meeting is just a group of individuals with unique thoughts and beliefs coming together to find common agreements. They meet to find the thoughts and beliefs that they share and together create the company culture. Each of them wants to move forward into success. Perhaps they need to decide the direction of the corporation, how to market a new product or simply when the company party will be held. Everyone attending steps into the room with his or her own agenda and list of dislikes and must-haves. Everyone also enters the room with a memory and opinion about all the past encounters with the other attendees. "Is Peter going to be there? I hope not. His suggestions are always so conservative, stupid and boring." "Alice is such an airhead. I still can't forgive her for screwing up my project." "Chet is so lazy and negative." Almost everyone has these. These are Social NITs. Negative Intrusive Thoughts aimed at others. Most attendees don't have their attention focused on the task at hand. They are thinking about the others in the meeting or the work they should be doing; how to cover up their yawn; what's for dinner or how to avoid the next meeting.

So how do you, as enlightened business meeting leader, armed with Energy Tools, hold a meeting that is fun and enjoyable, task-oriented, short and successful? There are plenty of manuals out there that tell you how to run a productive business meeting. This may be the first one that suggests ways to prepave for one from a non-physical perspective. What I'm about to explain can be applied to any situation that you know will soon be arriving in your life. It could be a date, a conversation with your son, a shopping trip, a vacation, a new art project or a dinner party. The same tools and techniques apply to any upcoming event. We'll just use the situation of a business meeting to illustrate the tool here.

Whether you are leading the meeting or are a participant, this event is FOR you. It has entered your life experience to offer you something. At the very least, it is here to give you the opportunity to hold your boundaries and maintain your energy and balance – no matter what happens during the meeting. Only from a foundation of balance can you make the meeting work for you. Remember the meetings you've attended where an attendee (or even the leader) has lost his balance and has become affected by the others around him? Perhaps the company bully challenged him or the boss asked a question he hadn't prepared for. Remember how he stumbled painfully and perhaps never really regained his balance. Once this happens, it can be difficult to continue with Certainty and Ease. Energy Tools will assist when you find yourself in this position. They work even more effectively if you use them prior to the meeting, to set the tone. In fact, that is what this is all about. You are creating a life experience that feels good and fun and supports YOU, no matter what happens beyond your Octahedron. Everything beyond your boundaries is Shakespeare's theatre.

This doesn't mean you will become a controlling, insensitive, greedy bully, insisting everyone do it your way. In fact, just the opposite occurs. By Prepaving prior to the meeting, staying "in your space," holding your boundaries and keeping your crown at Certainty, the desired results unfold in an extremely amusing and stress-free way. You also allow the other attendees to have a great time and reach their goals too. It's win-win for everyone. Okay-let's play.

Choose an event that will occur within the next week or two. Choose something that is relatively easy already, an event that you may feel some anticipation toward, but not a tremendous amount of anxiety. In other words, don't choose the yearly evaluation interview for your first experiment. It's more important that you practice on the easy challenges before you tackle the Big Kahuna. Success happens more smoothly if you take it in small increments, acclimate to your new surroundings and then take another step. Jumping off the cliff all at once is an option *and* it can come with a larger-than-life Growth Period. Be easy on yourself. This isn't a race.

So let's say you will be conducting your department's monthly communications meeting, a meeting no one really enjoys attending, yet is the only opportunity all members have to quickly update each other on the status of individual projects that affect everyone. This tool also works if you are a participant and want to experience an easy, successful meeting.

Energy Tool #16
Prepaving

This is to be done a day or two prior to the meeting:

1. Set aside an hour to do this work. Sit quietly where you won't be disturbed. Find the Center of Your Head and clear it out by placing any intruding people or thoughts into your Grounding Line or use Making Separation Roses. This is not an analytical process, so when your analyzer begins Yes-Butting and the NITs begin to chatter, ask your analyzer to sit outside or flip the switch in the Center of Your Head to "Off." This time is for you.

2. Run the rivers of energy through your body. The quieter you get before you begin, the more success you'll experience.

3. From the Center of Your Head, imagine a bubble in front of you.

4. Within this bubble, imagine the empty meeting room. Attach Grounding Lines to all eight corners. Command them to release any energy that might already be in the room that won't support success.

5. Visualize a large Golden Ball above the room. Ask it to fill the space with gold, neutrality and balance.

6. Set the tone of the meeting at a pleasant color. To do this, choose a color that feels best to you at the present moment. Red and black probably aren't good choices. Sky blue and gold are always winners.

Create a giant Rose in the center of the room with this color as the blossom and a stem that goes into the earth.

7. Begin to throw aspects that you'd like to experience during the meeting into the giant Rose. Possibilities include: permission, amusement, equality, abundance, kindergarten, success, honesty warmth, focus, camaraderie, plenty of time, good jokes and ease.

8. Create a clone of this Rose at the entry door. This serves as a decompression Rose, assisting all who walk through it to leave the rest of the world behind.

9. Imagine the attendees entering the room, one at a time. As they enter say, "Hello" and take a moment with each one individually. Invite them to have a seat.

10. Put a Grounding Line on each attendee and ask the Line to release any energy that keeps his or her attention not in present-time. It is not necessary to get into specifics here. Do this all from the Center of Your Head and at neutral. If you find yourself becoming charged, judgmental or off-balance, simply take a moment, breathe, check your energy channels and return to a place of neutrally. Watch the movie unfold before you. This won't work if you are charged or negative in any way.

11. Deliberately think of one thing you appreciate about each person. Keep it simple and easy.

12. Now imagine you're in the meeting room. Ground yourself and give yourself a Golden Ball of Light.

13. Visualize the top of your head at a color that represents Certainty to you. Imagine the word Certainty written there. If another word is more appropriate, substitute that one.

14. Visualize the meeting in progress. Just make it up. Imagine everyone enthusiastic, creative and participatory. Imagine only the best. Don't get stuck on making it perfect or realistic. That's your Analyzer stepping in again.

15. This is your Bedroom Fantasy Tool in a slightly different setting. As you work, you may notice your own NITs come up and out. Simply Ground them or collect them in a Rose and blow them up. They are only your old belief patterns and limiting thoughts that are rushing to the surface to be released.

16. When you feel complete or the imaginary meeting comes to a conclusion, visualize everyone leaving the meeting room in high spirits, successful and enthusiastic.

17. Re-Ground the bubble of the meeting room.

18. Make the bubble gold.

19. Pop it and watch all the bits and fragments disappear.

20. Remember a time when you felt successful and grateful. Feel those feelings now.

21. Your Prepaving is complete. You may fill up with your own Golden Ball of Light and continue your day.

On the day of the meeting:

1.   Find your quiet space again and be in the Center of Your Head, at neutral.

2.   Recreate the bubble with the room in it and the meeting in-progress.

3.   Re-Ground the room and fill it with gold again.

4.   Re-set or change the color of the Roses.

5.   Look around and notice what you notice.

6.   Ground yourself, re-set your crown at Certainty.

7.   When all is as you like it, make the bubble gold.

8.   Pop it and watch all the bits and fragments disappear.

9.   Remember a time when you felt Gratitude. Feel that now.

10. Fill up with your own Golden Ball of Light.

11. Step into the meeting with a Grounding Line attached, your crown at Certainty and Success, your Octahedron in place or your Rose in front of you.

12. Notice with amusement if anyone in the meeting recognizes all the gear you have strapped on your body and smile!

•••

Several years back we consulted with a company that produced a product that was delivered on a monthly basis. Although they had been in business for over 20 years, they were experiencing financial difficulties. Ten months, nine group classes and 15 individual sessions later, the company began to flourish. They increased their buyers and therefore income by 50% and the quality of the finished product was greatly improved. Many of the employees became happy and found themselves doing things they thought they never would. One bought a house, another got married, several joyfully left and were replaced by more capable and well-matched people.

When we completed our work, however, and left them to continue using the tools and processes we'd introduced, the growth reached a plateau. "What happened?" several of the more enthusiastic employees asked us. What happened was the owner of the company stopped using the Energy Tools himself and discontinued incorporating them in his business. He began instead to allow his old thoughts and beliefs of lack and limitation to seep into his belief structure and his company. The next step of the company's success would have included an expansion into larger offices. That never happened. The company is still more successful than it ever was, but they are no longer growing and expanding. The glass ceiling they keep hitting is the owner's limiting beliefs.

A testimonial to the widespread appeal of these simple tools is the story of one of our students who is also an attorney.

Jack began this case two years ago and it involved very emotional issues. A nursing care facility was suspected of neglecting elderly patients. The case was very complicated and political. Eighteen months into the case and before the second appeal, Jack began learning these Energy Tools. Back then Jack was a "typical" lawyer in many ways. He did however, have a big heart. He also possessed the usual level of skepticism and resistance many people have when they begin new adventures. Because of this skepticism, Jack didn't intentionally use his Energy Tools for his business. He only applied them to his personal life. You see, back then, Jack had a strong belief that the settlement he was asking for wouldn't be granted. That large amount had never *previously* been granted in his county.

It wasn't until the start of the second trial that Jack began to, very methodically, use his Energy Tools for Prepaving. Jack had a strong, emotional desire for justice for the neglected elders. He wanted these folks healed and helped. Jack worked his tools. He saw this as another opportunity for growth and personal integration.

Our class meeting after the trial found Jack extremely excited and talkative. Not only did his client win the case, she received more compensation than had ever been granted in this county!

•••

What you allow yourself to imagine, think and believe IS possible in life and in business. The degree of your success is absolutely determined by the degree to which you imagine you can succeed.

In Conclusion ~ Jim

Mastering Alchemy Creating Heaven on Earth

Alchemy is not magic; however, it does produce very wonderful and magical results. When you are aligned, Alchemy is the Universal Wisdom that nurtures creations into tangible reality. It is the Science of Spirituality. It is the dance that weaves the universal elements into conscious form. Using the tools in this book is the first step in mastering Alchemy.

By first accepting and then understanding that all things are possible, you are then able to intentionally transform one possibility into another. By learning to simply change one vibrational thought, feeling or belief into another, you will begin to understand how to create and sustain Well-Being, Abundance and Joy, effortlessly. Difficult? No! Easy? Actually, much easier than you might think.

So what is Alchemy? The definition I received from the Archangels, Ascended Masters and Teachers of Light whom I work with is:

The ability to change the frequency of thought, alter the harmonics of matter and apply the elements of Love to create a desired result.

Let's start simply. For example, if you wish to have water available to drink, it is useful to have a container to hold the water. Similarly, to hold the wisdom of Alchemy for your creations, you must also have a container. The aura is an electromagnetic field surrounding you, but it has lost its definition or structure. It is the water without a container. By changing your pattern of thought and restructuring the harmonics of the aura to form one of the sacred geometric fields, (such as the Octahedron, Star Tetrahedron or Cube), the container is created. Depending upon your level of awareness, each of these ancient, sacred geometric shapes align with a unique, higher dimensional body of wisdom. The geometry becomes an antenna, both a transmitter and a receiver.

The aura without structure and focus is like a radio that cannot lock onto a station. By creating a specifically tuned transmitter and receiver, you start to tune this Personal Energy Field to your own frequency. This allows you to tune out incoherent frequencies that constantly flow through you. These disruptive frequencies don't belong to you and have nothing to do with your purpose. Many of these are misaligned with who you are but hold such strong magnetic charge that they actually blind you to your understanding of your purpose.

Once this geometric container is in place, fascinating new opportunities become available. For example, by learning to increase the speed at which the Octahedron spins, you begin to rise above life's dramas, noise and distraction. This creates an opportunity to realign your antenna to your purpose and maybe even become happy, passionate and enthusiastic!

To take this to the next step, it is possible to increase the spin of the field to approaching the "Speed of Light." At this faster vibration, the range of reception and awareness expands, accessing many levels of higher dimensional consciousness. This is much like increasing the quality of your radio so you are able to tune into and enjoy a greater range of music.

Sound difficult? It is NOT! Again, this is easier than you may think. It simply requires the intention and desire to Know yourself and the Source of your creation.

This Personal Power Field holds the wisdom of Alchemy. It holds all that is required to turn the lead of ignorance into the gold of personal awareness. By fine-tuning this Octahedron, or antenna, you will eliminate the noisy, incoherent frequencies of events and people around you and begin to Know Yourself.

This fine-tuned alignment provides a new quiet focus. You begin to remember and rewire yourself in ways that have not been available for many life times, allowing you to receive, remember and re-experience the wisdom that you already know in the higher dimensions.

Here is where the magical results begin. From this new, higher, faster perspective you will find that Time exists in a very different form. There is no past or future. There is only Now. In this Now, known as Simultaneous Time, all experiences exist at the same moment in the same place. In this simultaneous NOW, the answer to any question is available to you before you have to act or respond to the question. Not only are the answers available, but the results of those answers can also be completely known before you act. Think about this! If you knew all the answers and what would happen in each situation before you had to act, then why would you ever chose an experience that was not enjoyable? With total choice, you would choose the possibility that most joyfully met your needs and then step into that choice, creating the reality you desire.

From this higher, faster, stabilized form of consciousness, you become aware that many of the concepts, beliefs and truths once held in this lower consciousness are no longer accurate or useful in the higher perspective. You now have the opportunity to make new choices. You can choose to play the game you have always played, or you can step up to a greater platform of certainty, seniority, personal power, happiness, command and grace. On this platform you will find that you have many more colors on your pallet to choose from. The pictures you paint with this pallet will be much more grand and alive. And by simply reconstructing a sentence or speaking with a different tone, you will create experiences with very different results. By changing the frequency of thought, altering the harmonics of matter and applying the elements of Love, you will create the results of your Dreams.

If this sounds like wishful thinking or fantasy, it is not. It is a simple doorway that has been hidden by the noise of the game, the push and shove, right and wrong, good and bad of the third dimension. It is a doorway that leads to merging with the Soul, walking with the Archangels, learning to create with the Great Rays of Creation and much, much more.

It is time to awaken and become who you are as a citizen of the Higher Dimensions.

As the veils of ignorance and forgetfulness are being dissolved, many wonderful teachers, leaders and healers are awakening. And as YOU awaken, it will be your opportunity to awaken the others who are now stirring. Alchemy is your natural state of wisdom. Mastering Alchemy is the means to create Heaven on Earth.

Many blessings to you,

Jim

In Conclusion ~ Roxane

Be Who You Came Here to Be

Two groups of spiritual warriors found themselves in a very real and important dilemma. They understood their personal, spiritual missions and recognized that energy existed that could prevent them from completing their work. They asked the Creator for the tools they needed, and each warrior received the package as requested.

Each package contained three items: a sword, a shield, and body armor. The sword represented Truth and could never be broken. The shield represented Knowledge of the weakness of the destructive energy, and Knowledge from the ancients. The body armor represented spiritual awareness and the Wisdom to wield the Truth (sword) and hold up the Knowledge (shield) in the face of a challenge.

Soon the challenging energy became evident and both groups of Spiritual Warriors felt they were ready. The first group opened their packages and stared with disbelief. Everything was in parts! There was a manual that said, "SOME ASSEMBLY REQUIRED." They couldn't prepare in time, and were quickly overrun and defeated by the intruders. They blamed Creator, each other and "the world." They never learned to use their tools.

The other group had opened their packages long ago. They had put their tools together and had practiced with them. It was a good thing they did, for they found the sword to be almost too fast and sharp to handle properly. The shield had so many options, they had difficulty knowing exactly how to hold it, and the body armor was very heavy! With practice, intention and meditation, they eventually learned how to balance everything, and they were ready.

They soon realized that no single tool worked without all three being engaged. The body armor was the key, for it gave them the wisdom to control the sword and the shield. When the challenging energy arrived, it took one look at this strong, well-prepared force and fled. No tears were shed on either side and the battle never occurred. The group celebrated their victory! (9)

●●●

Finding and holding your Truth, your Knowledge and your Wisdom is now, more than ever, required, in order to stand strong within your circle of inner peace while you watch the changes unfold around you.

How can you be in this shifting world, yet not be affected by it? You must first *ask* for the spiritual tools that will best assist you. When these tools arrive, as in the parable, you must then *practice* using them until they are a natural extension of who you are, as natural as using a spoon or driving your car.

The simple Energy Tools you've just learned will assist you to thrive and serve in today's unfolding Shift. With these tools, you will "walk through the valley of the shadow of death and fear no evil." You will be who you came here to be, effectively able to assist and uplift others at the right time, at the right place, in the best way possible, without sacrificing your own truth.

We are all being called to step forward and lead, to fulfill our original spiritual intentions. The drama, noise and challenges we find ourselves in today are not economic or social or even political. These are spiritual tests. They test our private, personal commitment to do whatever it takes to be a leader and a clear channel that allows Love to flow through us, to others, unobstructed.

What an incredible time to be alive, practice your wisdom and be the Spiritual Leader you came here to be. These are important times, times that can be joyous and uplifting or rife with struggle and suffering. The choice is yours. Many are indeed choosing to struggle and believe they are victims. Many more of us are consciously choosing to hold our connection to the greater, wiser, older part of ourselves no matter what occurs around us. We are choosing to create a way of life filled with Certainty, Personal Power, Respect, Amusement, Command and Graciousness.

When you choose to use your Spiritual Tools, you will be able to respond and thrive, rather than react and doubt. You will be living a way of life, full of your Self.

And as you make that choice,
you will return

Home.

In Joy,
Roxane

References

(1) *The Alchemist,* Paulo Coelho.

(2) *Stopping: How to Be Still When You Have to Keep Going,* David Kundtz.

(3) *Abraham-Hicks Publications,* Jerry and Esther Hicks.

(4) *Patch Adams,* Universal Studios.

(5) *The Science of Innate Intelligence* (video), Life Enhancement Services. Bruce Lipton, Ph.D,

(6) The Presence of the Past: Morphic Resonance & the Habits of Nature, Rupert Sheldrake, Ph.D.

(7) *Reference Guide for Essential Oils,* Connie and Alan Higley, Abundant Health.

(8) *The Secret Dowry of Eve: Woman's Role in the Development of Consciousness,* Glynda-Lee Hoffmann.

(9) *The Parables of Kryon,* Lee Carroll and Kryon.

For more information about what Roxane Burnett offers please explore: **www.TransitionCoachingForWomen.com**.

For more information about what Jim Self offers please explore: **www.MasteringAlchemy**.

About the Authors

Roxane Burnett is a credentialed teacher and personal coach. She has been teaching tools for developing intuition and Personal Power to individuals, businesses and women's groups since 1994. She had a successful career as an art director for two large corporations and as manager of her own design firm. Her highly acclaimed lectures and seminars are sought throughout the country. Seminars include: *Spiritual Abilities and Tools for Intuition, Personal Energy Management, Spiritual Warrior Training,* and *Female Alchemy.* Roxane  has been featured on television, radio and in national publications both in the US and Australia.

Roxane can be reached by contacting Transition Coaching for Women. **www.TransitionCoachingForWomen.com.** She offers a free monthly e-zine free personal assessments and complimentary mini-coaching sessions.

Jim Self is often introduced as a teacher's teacher and a healer's healer. He has been leading seminars and teaching healing, clairvoyance and personal energy management courses throughout North America since 1980. Jim has been featured on television, radio and in inter-national publications.

Since childhood, Jim has retained a conscious awareness and ability to recall his experiences within the sleep state. Over the last ten years, this awareness has expanded into relationships with the Archangels, Ascended Masters and Teachers of Light. The information presented in the Mastering Alchemy Program is a co-creation of these relationships.

Jim walks with a foot in both worlds. At the age of twenty-six, he was elected to his first of two terms to the San Jose, CA City Council and later became the Vice Mayor. Before completing his second term, he was asked by President Jimmy Carter to be an advisor and the Director of Governmental Operations for the Dept. of Energy. As an entrepreneur, he has successfully built and sold two corporations, and is the founder and current board chairman of a third biomedical company.

Jim can be reached by contacting **www.MasteringAlchemy.com.**